well

well

LISA KRON

THEATRE COMMUNICATIONS GROUP
NEW YORK
2006

Well is published by Theatre Communications Group, Inc., 520 Eighth Avenue, 24th Floor, New York, NY 10018-4156.

This publication is made possible in part with public funds from the New York State Council on the Arts, a State Agency.

TCG books are exclusively distributed to the book trade by Consortium Book Sales and Distribution, 1045 Westgate Drive, St. Paul, MN 55114.

LIBRARY OF CONGRESS CATALOGING-IN-PUBLICATION DATA

Kron, Lisa.
Well / Lisa Kron. —1st ed.
p. cm.
Author's theatrical exploration of issues of health and illness both in the individual and in a community, by using her mother as an example.
ISBN-13: 978-1-55936-253-5
ISBN-10: 1-55936-253-7
1. Health—Drama. 2. Diseases—Drama. 3. Mothers—Diseases—Drama.
I. Title.
PS3561.R584W46 2006
812'6—dc22
2006006542

Book design and composition by Lisa Govan
Cover design by Mark Melnick

First Edition, March 2006
Second Printing, March 2010

ACKNOWLEDGMENTS

Well was developed over a period of five years. I am deeply grateful to the following people and institutions:

Charlotte Stoudt, Greg Leaming, Ellie Covan and Dixon Place, Jocelyn Clarke, Robert Blacker and the Sundance Institute Theatre Program, George C. Wolfe and The Public Theater, American Conservatory Theater, Long Wharf Theatre, Baltimore's CENTER-STAGE, New York Theatre Workshop, Hartford Stage, the NEA/TCG Theatre Residency Program for Playwrights and Creative Capital Foundation—the greatest funding and artists support organization EVER.

Nancy Blum, who continually pushed me to think bigger and deeper about this play.

All the generous and talented actors who enabled development of the piece along the way: Joanna P. Adler, Kenajuan Bentley, Saidah Arrika Ekulona, Lola Pashalinski, A-men Rasheed, Welker White, Joel Van Liew, and especially the great Jayne Houdyshell.

Peg Healey for her beautiful love, always.

Most particularly I would like to thank Leigh Silverman and John Dias. The structure of this play was developed through hours of brain-twisting conversation with these very brilliant collaborators. This play is as much theirs as it is mine.

And, last but not least, I thank my mother, Ann Kron, who allowed me to cause her great anxiety by turning her into a character in this play because, like the character Ann Kron, she values creativity above all, and so her curiosity about how this strange play might turn out overrode her sincere wish that I would write about something else. She is brave and generous and complicated in all the best ways. She is my inspiration. I hope this play is half as interesting as she is.

ACKNOWLEDGMENTS

vii

PREFACE

The style of *Well* developed out of an aesthetic collision I experienced in my formative years when I arrived in the East Village performance world in the mid-1980s, and my inherent appreciation for traditional theatrical structures was confronted with performances built on structures that ranged from nontraditional to nonexistent. The tension between my notions of how a play was supposed to look and the often electrifying free-for-alls I was witnessing formed in me the preoccupations that have shaped my work since.

I began my writing life by not writing at all, but by improvising humorous anecdotal stories on the many tiny stages that used to pepper the East Village. Initially my goals were to learn to make an authentic connection with an audience, to feel and shape the energy in a room and to teach myself the skills to make an audience laugh on a consistent basis. When I felt I was beginning to master those skills, I began to want to make something more complicated, more theatrical. And so I began the long and ongoing process of teaching myself how to make plays out of these stories. And fairly quickly I stumbled on the inherent flaw of the solo play—it's very difficult to create dramatic action when there is no second character onstage to provide an obstacle to the agenda of the primary character. The solution I came to in my solo plays, *101 Humiliating Stories* and *2.5 Minute Ride*, was to locate the action of the play not in the events of the stories being told, but instead in the very act of telling a story. I did not stand in front of an audience as an omniscient narrator, but instead created a character of myself with a transparent agenda about whom the audience could ask, "Who is this person and why is she telling me this story? What does she need out of this? What is going to happen to her in the course of this event we're watching?" The audience witnesses this character negotiate the volatile act of telling a story and lose her balance in the unpredictable dynamic between teller and listener. They see her get derailed from her agenda and ultimately break open, telling them something new, something she hadn't planned. An epigraph I often used in programs for *2.5 Minute Ride* is: "The first time you tell a story, it's fact. The second time, it's fiction." I wanted to theatrically delineate between the great story, which may appear to have a lot of suspense, but doesn't really because the teller is standing before you, safe and sound; and the moment something is first told, the moment of vulnerable revelation, the moment of not knowing the outcome or effect. This seemed to me to be theatrically exciting.

My home for my first ten years of performing in New York was the lesbian theater collective, the WOW Café. In my years at WOW I was taken apart as a know-it-all and put back together as something closer to an artist. I had come to New York with a basic undergraduate theater education and then I had toured for a season as an actor with a national repertory company, and I was pretty sure I had a handle on what worked onstage and what didn't. And then I came to WOW where theater was being made by people who had no theater background to speak of and were breaking the "rules" right and left because they weren't aware there were rules to break. WOW was organized on a sweat equity principle, so if you put in work on someone else's show you would be given time to do a show of your own. And over and over again in those first years I watched people request a slot for a show, and I would think, There's no way you can make a show. You don't know anything about how to make theater. And without fail, I would go to see their show and see something riveting. Of course most of the shows (including my own) were far from perfect. But what I remember about the theater I saw in those years is a series of the most extraordinary, appalling, entertaining, *dynamic* moments, which left me eternally fascinated with what happens on a stage when you put someone there who does not know the rules. It began to seem to me that this was a key to viscerally feeling the power of theater, and I began to employ a mechanism in my work of flipping back and forth in my relationship with the audience from being a performer on a stage to being a person in a room with many other people. I did this instinctively in my solo work, but as we've mounted productions of *Well* I've had to dissect this mechanism so that it could be explained to the actors in the ensemble. It's been fascinating to see how difficult it is for them to make sense of this concept in rehearsal, but how immediately they grasp it in performance as they feel the jolt of excitement that goes through the audience when the traditional performer/ audience relationship is subverted. It's a galvanizing moment in which everyone onstage and off- can feel the power of the interdependent bond between performer and audience. It's a theatrical conceit, of course, but it makes the audience feel the electricity of something happening right now in this moment in this theater, and it creates the delicious illusion that anything could happen next.

So the style of *Well* comes out of these preoccupations. The play is driven forward by the narrator, "Lisa," whose plan is to present a coherent performance in which she can make her points about illness and wellness. But the structure falls apart and in the fissures that rip through the planned play, authentic, unplanned encounters erupt instead. It feels like the entire play has gone off the tracks, but, in fact, the more things fall apart in *Well*, the more they are actually coming together, because *Well* is made of a number of small structures all contained inside a superstructure large enough to hold all the chaos and contradiction that has ensued. This superstructure is never really seen, but its effect is felt in the final moments of the play, when it becomes evident that both the form and the content of the play have all along been about making room enough to allow life to spill over in all its contradictory messiness.

By the way, it's a lot more fun than it sounds.

well

Production History

Well received its world premiere at The Public Theater (George C. Wolfe, Producer; Mara Manus, Executive Director) on March 16, 2004. The production was directed by Leigh Silverman; the set design was by Allen Moyer, the costume design was by Miranda Hoffman, the lighting design was by Christopher Akerlind, the sound design was by Jill BC Duboff; the dramaturg was John Dias and the stage manager was Martha Donaldson. The cast included:

Lisa Kron	LISA KRON
Jayne Houdyshell	ANN KRON

Ensemble

Joel Van Liew	HOWARD NORRIS, HEAD NURSE, HIMSELF
Saidah Arrika Ekulona	LORI JONES, KAY, MRS. PRICE, CYNTHIA, HERSELF
Welker White	JOY, DOTTIE, HERSELF
Kenajuan Bentley	JIM RICHARDSON, NURSE 2, LITTLE OSCAR, BIG OSCAR, HIMSELF

Well received its West Coast premiere at the American Conservatory Theater in San Francisco on February 11, 2005. The production was directed by Leigh Silverman; the set design was by Allen Moyer, the costume design was by Miranda Hoffman, the lighting design was by Christopher Akerlind, the sound design was by Garth Hemphill; the dramaturg was John Dias and the stage manager was Martha Donaldson. The cast included:

Lisa Kron   LISA KRON
Jayne Houdyshell   ANN KRON

ENSEMBLE

Joel Van Liew   HOWARD NORRIS,
                                                      HEAD NURSE, HIMSELF
Saidah Arrika Ekulona   LORI JONES, KAY, MRS. PRICE,
                                                         CYNTHIA, HERSELF
Welker White   JOY, DOTTIE, HERSELF
A-men Rasheed   JIM RICHARDSON, NURSE 2,
                              LITTLE OSCAR, BIG OSCAR, HIMSELF

Well opened on Broadway at the Longacre Theatre on March 30, 2006. It was produced by Elizabeth I. McCann, Scott Rudin, Boyett Ostar Productions, True Love Productions, Roger Berlind, John Dias, Terry Allen Kramer, Carole Shorenstein Hays and Joey Parnes (Executive Producer), in association with Larry Hirschhorn, The Public Theater and the American Conservatory Theater. It was directed by Leigh Silverman; the set design was by Tony Walton, the costume design was by Miranda Hoffman, the lighting design was by Christopher Akerlind, the sound design and original music were by John Gromada; the dramaturg was John Dias and the stage manager was Susie Cordon. The cast included:

Lisa Kron	LISA KRON
Jayne Houdyshell	ANN KRON

ENSEMBLE

John Hoffman	HOWARD NORRIS, HEAD NURSE, HIMSELF
Saidah Arrika Ekulona	LORI JONES, KAY, MRS. PRICE, CYNTHIA, HERSELF
Christina Kirk	JOY, DOTTIE, HERSELF
Daniel Breaker	JIM RICHARDSON, NURSE 2, LITTLE OSCAR, BIG OSCAR, HIMSELF

CHARACTERS

LISA KRON

New York performance artist writing a play NOT about herself.

ANN KRON

Late sixties/early seventies, Midwestern housewife, lethargic and in pain, yet surprisingly vibrant. Warm and funny.

THE ENSEMBLE

A group of four actors that Lisa has hired to be in the play. They are designated here as A, B, C and D, but should be referred to throughout the play by their actual names. As the "intended play" unravels and their "rehearsed" scenes are interrupted, we see that these "real people" have to grapple with the unexpected events onstage. As the play continues, we see their standard actor show-must-go-on ethic erode as they (like the audience) start to find Ann a more compelling source of information, entertainment and warm human connection.

- A, white woman, thirties/forties, plays Joy, Dottie and herself
- B, black woman, thirties/forties, plays Lori Jones, Kay, Mrs. Price, Cynthia and herself
- C, black man, twenties to fifties, plays Jim Richardson, Nurse 2 , Little Oscar, Big Oscar and himself
- D, white man, twenties to fifties, plays Howard Norris, Head Nurse and himself

Tonight.

THE SETTING

The setting for *Well* is the theater in which it's being performed. On one portion of the stage is a slice of Lisa's parents' living room, including a La-Z-Boy recliner in which Ann Kron is sleeping at the top of the show. Ann's area is cluttered, with shelves and tables and drawers filled with books, magazines, interesting collectibles, toys and knick-knacks . . . There is a staircase leading off to the second floor, and an exit leading off toward the kitchen and basement. The effect should be as if Lisa has plucked her mother out of her house, shaken off all she could, and then plopped her down onto the stage along with everything that stuck. The rest of the stage is flexible, allowing settings for the neighborhood and Allergy Unit scenes to assemble and disperse. As the "intended play" derails, this half of the stage should reflect the derailment with incomplete scene changes, broken and malfunctioning scenery, etc. The "special light" is literally a square of isolated light that Lisa retreats into when she feels it necessary to have a private conversation with the audience.

NOTE

There is a great deal of overlapping dialogue in the play. Where appropriate I have inserted double slashes (//) to indicate where the overlap of the next line should begin. Also, there are moments in the play where confusion ensues and a certain amount of ad-libbing is necessary. The purpose of this is to generate an authentic sense of commotion and disorientation. No ad-libbing of specific lines that can be distinguished by the audience is necessary.

Lights come up as Lisa enters and crosses to center stage. She carries a small stack of note cards. Ann Kron is sleeping in her La-Z-Boy recliner, stage left.

LISA *(To the audience)*: Hello. Good evening. Hi. Thank you all so much for coming. I want to tell you a little bit about what we're going to be doing. This play that we're about to do deals with issues of illness and wellness. It asks the question: Why are some people sick and other people are well? Why are some people sick for years and years and other people are sick for a while but then they get better? Why is that? What is the difference between those people?

This play is *not* about my mother and me. That is my mother there in that La-Z-Boy recliner, which is where she spends most of her time because she doesn't feel well enough to get up and do other things—but this is not about her. It's not about how she's been sick for years and years and years and I was sick as well but somehow I got better. It's not about how she was able to heal a neighborhood but she's not able to heal herself. It's not *about* those things but it does use those things as a vehicle for *(Reads from the top note card)* "a multicharacter theatrical exploration of issues of health and illness both in the individual and in a community."

ANN *(Groaning, still asleep)*: Oh dear lord.

LISA *(Reacting in sudden irritation to her mother's unexpected interruption)*: Mom!! *(She recovers, slightly embarrassed by her own outburst)* I'm sorry. What is that thing about being around your parents that makes you act like a thirteen year old? Do you know what I mean? You grow up and you start your own life, and you move away and you do therapy and you get some distance. And after a while you start to be able to see your family so clearly. And you think: Wow, the next time I go home I am really going to be able to help them out. But then when you get home, what you realize is that your parents live in an alternate universe where your therapy has no power. Do you know what I mean? They're in a whole different reality. When I am in my reality it is so clear that there are things my mother could do to get better. I mean, I was sick as well and I got better, so I know it can be done. But then I get back here and—but this is not about me and her. This is a theatrical exploration of issues which are universal and for which we will occasionally be using my mother as an example. Which is why I have brought her here.

This is my mother.

(To Ann) Mom?

(Ann wakes up, groggy.)

ANN *(To Lisa)*: Hi.

LISA: Mom, how're you doing?

ANN: Oh lord. I'm having such a bad allergy day. I just can't focus on anything. I think there's a storm front coming in and I can't seem to hold my eyes open. I couldn't even get through the paper. Of course I didn't get any sleep today because the phone started to ring at about ten o'clock this morning and people kept calling all through my prime sleeping hours so . . . Oh, darn it, did I forget to tape the ice-skating? Criminy nitwit! I can't believe it! Oh, I think I set the VCR upstairs to tape it.

(Ann gets up. She sees the audience.)

Oh, hello. *(To Lisa)* You didn't tell me there were people here. *(Back to the audience)* Hi. How're you doing? I'd offer you a more comfortable chair but then where would we put the coats? Lisa, why don't you offer these people something to drink? I've got to go up and check that VCR. *(Goes upstairs, painfully limping on every step)* Oh lord, this hip is just . . . Oh! I don't know . . .

LISA   *(Watches her mother climb the stairs; then to the audience)*: My mother's been sick, like that, for as long as I can remember. For her whole life actually. Well, I come from a family where everyone is ill. It is the norm. The presumption of illness is so strong that it's the way we keep time. People in my family say things like, "Now I know for a fact the warranty's not up on that dishwasher. I got it the winter I had congestive heart failure seven times." Some of the people in my family have recognizable, identifiable illnesses like cancer and heart disease, diabetes . . . When I fill out forms with family medical history sections where you check off the little boxes, I check them all. Then there is the family mystery illness—the general inability to move, to physically cope, to stay awake. This is the primary malady suffered by my mother. My mother attributes her condition to "allergies." To my mother allergies are a highly underrated, sinister, life-destroying force that is kept secret from us by the evil AMA-controlled medical establishment. These days her condition would probably be labeled chronic fatigue syndrome or fibromyalgia or one of those but whatever it is—

W
E
L
L

🦶

ANN *(Returning)*: Well, I didn't tape it up there either.

LISA *(Continuing)*: . . . it has sapped all of her energy since she was a little girl.

ANN: I'm just disgusted. Did you offer these people something to drink?

LISA: They're fine.

ANN: Lisa, what's wrong with you? What would you people like?

(She leaves again, exiting toward the kitchen/basement. She yells back to the audience:)

Let me see what we've got.

LISA: Mom, they don't need a drink. They're fine.

ANN *(Offstage)*: Okay, we have, uh, Coke and some Diet Coke and Vernors—

LISA: Mom, they don't—

ANN *(Offstage)*: . . . root beer, if anyone wants that. I don't know if any of this stuff is still good.

LISA: Mom—

ANN *(Offstage)*: You know, I buy this stuff when it's on sale and then it just sits here and sits here and then when you need it it's bad.//There's something here, some kind of fruit . . . nectar that Elisabeth brought from Holland . . . hmm. I don't think I'd have the nerve to try that . . .

LISA *(To the audience, overlapping with Ann, above)*: Okay, people? No drinks. Okay? We're not going to complicate this thing with drinks.

(Ann returns, carrying a crumpled Meijer's grocery bag.)

ANN *(To the audience)*: Okay. What'll you have?

LISA *(To Ann)*: They're good.

ANN: Really?

LISA: Yup.

ANN: Okay, well, suit yourselves. I found these down there.

(She takes little individual packages of chips or party mix or cookies out of the bag and begins to throw them into the audience. She knows this is funny. There's a quality about her that's almost impish.)

I found them at that restaurant supply place. Aren't they cute? *(To Lisa)* Here.

(She throws one at Lisa. It hits her and falls. Ann is delighted.)

You don't want one? They're so cute.

(She throws another one and hits Lisa again.)

Okay. Suit yourself.

(Ann reaches behind her chair and gets a "grabber." She limps over to Lisa and snatches the snack packs off the floor with the grabber, then drops them back into her crumpled bag. She is delighted with herself.)

It's my grabber.

(She limps back out toward the kitchen/basement.)

LISA *(To the audience)*: My mother is a fantastically energetic person trapped in an utterly exhausted body. It's very confusing. Her energy level has two settings: all or nothing. Most of the time it's nothing, but when she has a burst of energy it's awe-inspiring. For instance, when we were very young she decided she wanted my brother and me to be raised in a racially integrated neighborhood, and then she set about to create one.

(Ann returns.)

ANN *(To Lisa)*: Ugh. I'm going to be so sorry I didn't wait till later to take that diuretic. *(Falls into her La-Z-Boy; then slightly suspicious)* What's going on?

LISA *(With total innocence)*: In what sense do you mean?

ANN *(The thought just occurring to her)*: You're not writing a play about me are you?

(Throughout this section, Lisa does her sincere, though ever so slightly condescending best, to walk her mother through these complicated concepts.)

LISA: Mom, we've talked about this before. I don't really write traditional plays. I work more in the genre of solo performance.

ANN: Okay. This solo performance, is it about me?

LISA: Well, this piece actually is not a solo. There are other people in it. It's like a solo show with other people in it. It's a whole new thing.

ANN: Wow, that sounds great. What is it about?

LISA: It is a *(Refers to note card)* "multicharacter theatrical exploration of issues of health and illness both in the individual and in a community." Did you want to read the grant proposal?

ANN: No. I just want to know what you're doing and if I need to go upstairs and hide until you're done. *(To the audience)* I don't even like to have my picture taken. I certainly don't want to be in a play. *(To Lisa)* So who's the individual?

LISA: Who?

ANN: That's what I'm asking.

LISA: What?

ANN: Lisa! You said you were writing something about health problems in an individual.

LISA: Yes. That's the issue being explored.

ANN: Okay. Who are you using to *explore* it?

LISA: I don't know what you mean by "using"?

ANN: Okay. What about the community?

LISA: What community?

ANN: You said something about a community.

LISA: The community! Well, let me tell you, Mom, the community is this neighborhood. It's about your work and how you helped to heal this neighborhood. And it also explores my time in the Allergy Unit at Henrotin Hospital.

ANN: Really?

LISA: Yes.

ANN: I suppose those are both important stories.

LISA: Yes they are. They're very important stories.

ANN: But now who's the individual?

LISA: The—

ANN: The individual.

LISA: Okay. Look. It's not *about* either one of us. I work using autobiographical material, but ultimately this is a theatrical exploration of a universal experience. So it does utilize some details about you, but, Mom, it's not that big of a deal.

ANN: All right, honey. It's okay. I just wanted to know what's going on. I don't like it, but I can deal with it. It's not like you're going to make it seem like I'm a hypochondriac or something. It's true I'm not really crazy about my living room ending up here, but I know you need to do your work. I don't want to make you self-conscious.

LISA *(Suddenly self-conscious)*: Thank you.

ANN *(Supportive)*: That's okay. You go ahead and do your thing.

LISA: Okay . . . *(Pause)* I'm going to be right back.

(Lisa steps into her "special light," and speaks confidentially to the audience:)

Just so you know, I'm aware that we're dealing with a couple of emotionally touchy topics here. There are certain things that we *(Meaning the audience and herself)* will be exploring for the purposes of this "exploration" that she and I have not actually ever talked about in life. In particular, my mother has a very different picture of what happened when I was a patient in the Allergy Unit and how and why I got better. And I don't intend to get into that with her here because that would be walking into a big emotional minefield and what is happening here is not about me having a big messy "carefrontation" with my mother. This is a "theatrical exploration of universal issues." But that's what is so incredibly helpful about this convention of interior monologue. It will allow *us* to explore these issues in a professional, theatrical context. And it will also make the process much easier on her. Because she's not a theater person, you know, so she doesn't quite get that there's a plan that's in motion here. But, you know what? It might make her a little more comfortable if I kind of keep her in the loop and explain things to her as we go along. Okay? Okay. Super.

(She steps out of the special light. To Ann:)

Okay, Mom. We're *(Meaning the audience and herself)* going to get going. And as I mentioned, we *(Meaning the audience and herself)* are going to be looking at some scenes back and forth from the neighborhood and from when I was in the Allergy Unit to see if we can find some resonances and some parallels between those stories of healing. Okay?

ANN: Yeah. Sure.

LISA: All right, then. Good.

(Commencing her "intended" play. To the audience:)

We're going to begin at Henrotin Hospital in Chicago. At the Allergy Unit. Which is where I went after withdrawing from college, when I was nineteen, in the winter of my junior year. The Allergy Unit was a place I had heard about all through my childhood, always spoken of in reverential tones. It was considered a haven. It was the one place they took allergies seriously, and going there was a milestone

I assumed was somewhere in my future—like a bat mitzvah. I'd had various symptoms since junior high school. But I did think I'd be able to make it through college first and//then go into the hospital—

ANN *(Interrupting Lisa)*: Junior high? Oh no. You were having problems long before that. *(To the audience)* Even in elementary school you could tell she was allergic. She had those big, dark circles under her eyes. "Allergic shiners" they call them.

LISA *(A bit stunned by the interruption, but picking up as if nothing has happened)*: . . . but that winter I couldn't keep up with my work. I couldn't finish the semester. I was shocked. I'd always been able to push through on willpower. But that winter I found myself with two options: Go into the Unit. Or watch my life derail. So—I went.

(Lisa crosses to the Head Nurse, who has entered along with the Allergy Unit setting.)

HEAD NURSE: Lisa, welcome to the Allergy Unit. Let's start you off with a quick tour. In there's the dayroom. A little on the shabby side I know. But of course, we can't use any new stuff because the off-gassing knocks most of our patients flat. No plastic anywhere on the Unit, of course. Wood, leather, cotton—all untreated when we can find it. Chem testing is in there. That's where we expose you to the various inhalants that might be causing your problem—perfume, newsprint, fabric softener. We won't go in there of course. If they're testing in there we don't want to let those fumes out. That'd be bad.

LISA *(To the audience)*: And when I got to the Unit I was confused and miserable. Because I was a nineteen-year-old college student, and almost all of the other patients on the Unit were middle-aged ladies. And I remember thinking to myself: I am sick, and you are sick, but I am not like you.

HEAD NURSE: So let's head on down to your room—

W
E
L
L

KAY *(Entering)*: Hello!

HEAD NURSE: Kay! How are you feeling, dear?

KAY: Oh! Tired. Sore. Happy.

HEAD NURSE: I'll bet. I heard that was quite a reaction.

KAY: Oh, it was. I just can't believe it. I know what it is now. I'm not crazy. *(Filled with joy and amazement)* I'm not crazy.

HEAD NURSE: Kay, that is super-duper. That's what we like to hear. This is Lisa, by the way. She just got here.

LISA: Hi.

KAY: Lisa, hello. Welcome. This is a fantastic place. You're going to get a lot of help here. Oh, I just feel GREAT.

(Kay exits.)

HEAD NURSE: Kay tested strawberries this morning. She had a psychotic break and tried to crawl through the air-conditioning vents. Okay, so follow me to your room.

(They arrive in Joy's room, where Joy is sitting on her bed.)

Knock, knock. Joy? Hi. Hi. I've got your new roommate here. This is Lisa.

LISA: Hello.

JOY: Hello. Lisa? Is it? I'm Joy.

LISA: Joy. Hi.

HEAD NURSE: Okay, Lisa. Have a seat and let's go over the next few days. As you know, the first order of business is to clear out your GI tract. And in order to do that you're going to be fasting.

LISA: For how long?

HEAD NURSE: Oh, depends . . . until you get clear—five, six days is average.

JOY: It took me eleven days to get clear.

HEAD NURSE: To move that along we're going to be giving you milk of magnesia, and then, in a couple of days we'll get going on the enemas.

JOY: Um-hmm.

HEAD NURSE: And every time you have a bowel movement you're gonna wanna give one of the nurses a ring to come in and have a look.

JOY: So they can see when you get clear.

HEAD NURSE: It's amazing what comes out of there. You are not going to believe how many layers of ancient gunk can pile up there in your intestine, but you'll see. It's actually kind of cool.

JOY: It's really interesting.

LISA: Okay.

HEAD NURSE: Here are your forms for the food testing. *(Hands her the forms)* Before you test a water or a food, you take your baseline pulse and you write that number here. And then you drink or eat whatever you're testing and you take your pulse again after ten minutes, twenty, forty and sixty. And you describe your reactions you have here and rate them from okay, meaning no reaction, to plus-one, -two, -three and -four.

JOY: With plus-four being the most severe.

HEAD NURSE: Let me show you here in Joy's book. Yeah, now see how Joy has done this . . . plus-four, plus-four, plus-three, plus-four. Wow, Joy, you've had a tough week!

JOY: Yeah, um. *(Murmuring)* Oh boy. Oh boy. This is not good.

(Joy takes her own pulse. She works very hard to maintain her composure.)

HEAD NURSE: What's up, Joy? Are you okay?

JOY *(Her panic and agitation levels are rising, but she tries to maintain a pleasant demeanor)*: The . . . um . . . no, it's fine . . . just, uh . . .

HEAD NURSE: Are you having a reaction?

JOY *(Still endeavoring, though not very successfully, to cover her agitation)*: Um-hmm. Yes, maybe. I think so. I think it might be— *(Jerks her head toward Lisa, totally furious)* I'm going to go down to the dayroom.

HEAD NURSE: Do you want some alkali salts sent down?

JOY: Yes. I think so. Yes. Okay? Nice to meet you. Oh boy . . .

(Joy exits.)

LISA: Is she all right?

HEAD NURSE: She'll be fine. Chances are there's some auto exhaust in your hair from the trip.

LISA: Oh!

HEAD NURSE: No matter how many precautions we take, when the outside world comes in here it can be very hard. So, why don't we get you started on some milk of magnesia? How's that sound?

LISA: Sounds fantastic.

(The Head Nurse exits. Lisa suddenly decides to cross into her special light. She addresses the audience:)

Just in case I was not clear about this, at the time I went into the Allergy Unit I believed in allergies. In my family we believe in allergies. And I did. We're a family that believes in things. Like racial integration for instance. I would say, actually, the two main things we believe in as a family are allergies and racial integration. In the same way my mother believes that a host of symptoms often dismissed as psychosomatic—including her own inability to stay awake—are really caused by allergies; she also believes in the positive effects of racial integration. It's important to be different, she says. If you're a part of the main group all the time, you never learn to see the world from anyone's point of view but your own. Okay. I just wanted to clarify that.

(Lisa steps out of the light. She begins the next part of the "exploration":)

From the time I was seven to the time I was fourteen—
(Suddenly breaking this introduction) Hold on. *(To Ann)*
Mom? This is where we introduce your work with the
Neighborhood Association.

ANN: Oh really? Oh good.

LISA *(Back to the audience)*: From the time I was seven to the time
I was fourteen, my mother was the president of the West
Side Neighborhood Association.

*(Neighborhood meeting assembles. Various neighbors from Lisa's
childhood speak to young Lisa or reenact a montage of neighborhood meetings, as Lisa continues to address the audience.)*

JIM: Hello, Lisa. Cynthia's here. She's out on the playground.
Bridget's out there too. Right, Howard?

HOWARD: Yep. But you're in charge of the coffee. Right, Lisa? You
always do a very nice job setting up the coffee and cookies.

JIM: Oh yes!

LISA: In 1968, when my mother started the Association, our
neighborhood in Lansing, Michigan, was in serious trouble. Terminally ill, most people assumed. My mom said
that was self-fulfilling prophecy.

MRS. PRICE: Hello, Lisa. Look at you!

LISA: She started suggesting to people that not only was the
West Side not sick, but that an integrated neighborhood
was actually healthier than a nonintegrated neighborhood.
And that an organization that was convinced of that could
stop the downward slide.

MRS. PRICE: Every time I see you, you get fatter and fatter. Why
is that? Why you getting so fat? Hmm?

LISA: It never occurred to my mother she'd end up running it.
She didn't have any political experience. Besides, she said
she was not well enough to take something like that on.

DOTTIE: Lisa, honey, did you see which way your mom went? I've
got to show her these dittos before I run them off. Oh!
I cannot keep track of her.

LISA: Over that seven years I sit in the back of a million meetings. I watch. I master the art of turning a Styrofoam cup
inside-out, which you can do if you push in from the bot-
tom just a little at a time.

JIM: The City of Lansing and the real-estate industry believe this
neighborhood is sick and is going to die because in their
minds there's no such thing as an integrated neighborhood.

MRS. PRICE: That's right. They're convinced neighborhoods
come in only three types: black, white or changing.

DOTTIE: Well, absolutely. I'm astonished at how often realtors
knock on our door trying to scare us into selling by "warn-
ing" us about the instability of this neighborhood.

JIM: There's lots of money to be made on a wave of panic selling.

HOWARD: I might mention that if you've looked at Jim's lawn
and looked at mine you might start to wonder which one
of *us* is the threat to property values.

LISA: The houses in this neighborhood are beautiful. The streets
are curvy. There are flowers on the boulevards. When the
first black families moved in, the city sent crews to dig the
flowers up.

MRS. PRICE: Two of our schools have already been closed and the
school board has slated four more for closing which will
leave the West Side without a single neighborhood school.

DOTTIE: It's my understanding that Saint Joe Park is being
offered to Oldsmobile for railroad sidings. Is that right?

LISA: That's the way it works, my mom says. That is how a slum
is made. It's not that the people who live in the neighborhood aren't taking care of themselves. The city withdraws
all the resources.

JIM: All right, so, Ann, you think we should start an organization? You know this kind of thing has been tried before.

LISA: My mom's idea is that the thing that will make this organization work where others have failed will be the use of
social activities.

MRS. PRICE: Social activities?

JIM: Oh, Ann.

HOWARD: Oh, Ann.

DOTTIE: Oh, Ann.

LISA: At first people are skeptical.

JIM: That's a sweet idea but people are very jealous of their time, Ann.

LISA: They think she's really naive.

HOWARD: Those kinds of things are a heck of a lot of work.

LISA: My mother says that it is a lot of work to organize all the volunteers to make the Christmas caroling and baseball games and Fourth of July parades happen. But that it is fundamentally important.

JIM: Now, Ann, what's important is the political work.

LISA: My mother says that social activities will fuel the political work. She says nothing is going to make people invested in fighting for this neighborhood like the feeling that they are needed.

(That scene completed, the ensemble exits and the transition begins for the next planned scene. Lisa is interrupted by Ann as she heads into this next scene.)

ANN: Hey, could I talk to you for a second?

LISA: I guess.

ANN: Just—could you come over here?

LISA: What is it?

ANN: You're doing a lot more about the neighborhood, right?

LISA: Some more, yeah.

ANN: That seemed awfully compressed.

LISA: It was compressed. That was a montage.

ANN: Was that supposed to be Howard and Jim?

LISA: Sort of. *(Off Ann's skeptical look)* Mom, I know we're not getting into every detail, but what I'm aiming for is more the overall effect.

ANN: Overall effect.

LISA: Yeah.

ANN: Well, there were sure an awful lot of complications in seven years—but okay.

LISA: Yeah.

ANN: What else do you remember about that time?

(From Lisa's past, Lori Jones, ten years old, blasts in and intimidatingly confronts Lisa.)

LORI: Ooh! You think you're so big.

(Lori stomps off.)

ANN: Who was that?

LISA: I think it was . . . Lori Jones.

ANN: Is that that little girl who was so mean to you in grade school?

LISA: Uh-huh.

ANN: Oh my. Is she in your play?

LISA: Oh my God! I hope not!
         (Collecting herself. Getting things back on track) Uh . . . Mom . . . This next scene takes place in the Allergy Unit.

(Nurse 2 comes to meet Lisa as the Allergy Unit setting assembles. He has a glass of water on a tray.)

NURSE 2: Ah, Lisa, here you are. Ready to do a water test?

LISA: What do I have to do?

NURSE 2: Drink this water.

LISA: And then what's supposed to happen?

NURSE 2: Then you wait to see if you have a reaction to it.

LISA: To water.

NURSE 2: Sure. Hopefully you won't have to try too many before you find one that's safe. You can't start testing food until you find a safe water.

LISA *(Tasting the water)*: Umm. Delicious.

NURSE 2: So head back to your room and fill out the testing form. All right, then. Good luck.

LISA: Thanks.

(Nurse 2 exits. Lisa goes to her bed, takes out her journal. Kay and Joy enter. They watch Lisa. Finally Joy speaks:)

JOY: So, Lisa, how did you find out about the Unit?
LISA: My mother knew about it.
KAY: Oh, you have a supportive family. *(To Joy)* That is so rare.
JOY: Yes it is.
KAY: You are really lucky, Lisa. How did your mother find out about it?
LISA: She saw it on *The Phil Donahue Show*.

(Kay and Joy both give a little gasp of recognition.)

KAY: Oh, I saw that. It was good—
JOY *(Overlapping a bit)*: That was very good.

(Beat.)

KAY *(To Lisa)*: So, what kinds of symptoms do you have?
LISA: I don't have any symptoms, actually. I'm just here for the enemas.
KAY: What?
LISA: Never mind.
KAY: Okay. I didn't get it. Was that a joke?
JOY *(Confidentially, to Kay)*: I think Lisa's experiencing some withdrawal right now.
KAY: Oh, right. The first days are so hard.
LISA *(Slightly irritated)*: I'm fine, actually.
KAY *(Sympathetic)*: Oh yeah. I'll bet once you're cleared out you're going to feel a whole lot better.
LISA: I'm fine.
JOY *(Noticing that Lisa is wringing her hands)*: Did you know that wringing your hands is an allergic symptom?
LISA *(Opens her hands and puts them down in her lap)*: No, I did not know that.

KAY: I've never had that but I do have restless leg.

JOY: Oh, I've heard about that.

KAY: Oh! It's a nightmare. *(To Lisa)* What are your symptoms again?

LISA: I have trouble staying awake.

KAY: Oh yeah yeah. That's very common.

LISA: And I have some concentration problems: focus . . . difficulties . . . that kind of thing.

KAY: So common.

JOY: Very, very common.

KAY: Do you have night terrors?

LISA: No.

KAY: I have night terrors. Are you really sensitive to loud noises?

LISA: I don't like loud noises.

KAY: That's allergy. Do you have hair loss? No, I can see you don't have hair loss. Joy does. Do you have chest pains? Joy has terrible chest pains.

(On the other side of the stage, Ann tries, not successfully, to get up quietly.)

ANN *(To Lisa)*: Sorry. Is it okay if I run up . . . ?

(A, who plays Joy, and B, who plays Kay, hang suspended mid-scene, not sure what to do.)

LISA: Yeah, it's fine.

ANN: Damn diuretic.

(Ann goes upstairs. A and B are momentarily flummoxed, but Lisa gives a very slight, willful nod, indicating that they are to continue with the scene.)

KAY *(Picking up where she left off)*: I know you're scared, sweety. But you're lucky to be here. The doctors here believe you when you tell them what's wrong.

JOY: Yes.

KAY: They listen to you and they believe you.

(Kay and Joy exit. Lisa introduces the next neighborhood scene, which replaces the Allergy Unit setting behind her during this speech.)

LISA *(To the audience)*: My two best friends are Oscar and Cynthia. Oscar lives next door on that side and Cynthia lives next door over there. The neighborhood is integrated, but by demographic chance my brother and I are the only white kids in our school. We're also the only Jews in our school. We're the only Jews in the whole neighborhood. We are the only Jews in our family, as a matter of fact, since my mother converted to marry my father, and my father left Germany by himself, and he doesn't have any relatives anymore, which makes us feel incredibly special (in spite of the assumption in the Midwest that although you might be a Jew, you're also still a Christian. Judaism, you know, is viewed in the Midwest as a kind of an accessory that you wear on top of your Christianity). In any case, it's a good thing to be different, my mother says. But I'm not so different from Oscar and Cynthia. We play together every day. Our favorite game is Singing Group, which is not a game that involves any singing. It involves standing on Oscar's picnic table and deciding which singing group we're going to be.

OSCAR: Ooh, I know. Y'all, let's be The Archies.

LISA: Yes! That's so cool! I love The Archies.

OSCAR: I'm'a be Archie.

LISA: Right. You be Archie. I'm'n'a be Veronica.

CYNTHIA *(Jumping up)*: Hey, y'all. I'm'a be Chaka Khan. Ooh, look at me. My boobies be hanging out all over the place. I'm swinging my bootie around . . .

LISA: We're being The Archies.

CYNTHIA: Okay, but I'm Chaka Khan. Oscar, you be Rufus.

OSCAR: That's bad. *(Meaning good)*

LISA: No! That person is not in The Archies!

OSCAR: This is better. It's Chaka Khan and Rufus. Come on.

LISA: No. I'm not playing that.

OSCAR *(Simultaneously with Cynthia)*: Come on.

CYNTHIA *(Simultaneously with Oscar)*: Why?

LISA: Because!

CYNTHIA: Ooh. She doesn't know Chaka Kahn and Rufus.

OSCAR: You don't know Chaka Kahn and Rufus?

CYNTHIA: Mm-hmm.

LISA: You guys, we have to pick a group we all know. *(Getting the best idea ever!!)* Let's be The Partridge Family.

OSCAR *(Simultaneously with Cynthia)*: The Partridge Family?

CYNTHIA *(Simultaneously with Oscar)*: The Partridge Family?

LISA: What's wrong with that?

OSCAR: The Partridge Family is bogue!

LISA: No!

OSCAR: Hold up. I gotta idea. I gotta idea. Lisa. You stand here, I'm'a stand there. This is a really good game. It goes like this. I call out like this: "Hey, white girl!" And you call me back, "Hey, black boy!" Okay? It's cool. It's a cool game.

LISA: Okay, you start.

OSCAR: Hey, white girl!

LISA: Hey, black boy!

CYNTHIA: That is cool.

(They all laugh.)

OSCAR: See?

(Ann returns from the upstairs bathroom. She speaks to some-one in the front row as the scene continues:)

ANN: They//used to do this thing of playing wedding out there. They had these complicated discussions about who was going to get to marry Otis—Carol or Lisa . . .

OSCAR: Hey, white girl!

LISA: Hey . . . *(To Ann)* Shhh! *(Back in scene)* . . . black boy!

(Ann continues talking.)

OSCAR: Hey, white girl!!

LISA: Hey, bla— *(To Ann)* Mom, please don't talk over the scene.*//*
(Back in scene) —black boy! . . .

ANN *(To Lisa)*: What? Oh, I'm sorry.

LISA *(To the audience)*: We continue in our loud, cool voices until
I hear my mother call me. I go into the back hall*//*where
I am informed gently . . .

ANN *(Continuing, to the audience)*: I sure hope she tells that wedding part—

LISA *(To Ann)*: Shhh! *(Back to the audience)* . . . but firmly that
"black boy" is a phrase I am not to use again. I state the
obvious: "But he is a black boy!" "Yes," she tells me, "but
that is a term that has been used historically to insult
black men and it's hurtful . . ."

ANN *(To the audience)*: I don't have the vaguest recollection of
saying that.*//(Simultaneously with Lisa, below)* I mean, it's
true but I don't remember saying anything like that . . .

LISA *(Simultaneously with Ann, above)*: "Oscar's not hurt by it! He
made up the game!" "Lisa, you cannot use that term." I go
back outside and I don't know what happens next. —Mom,
please!

ANN *(To Lisa)*: Oh. Shh. I'm sorry. *(To the actors playing Cynthia and
Oscar)* Hi there. How're you doing? *(Gets up to cross to them)*

LISA: Mom!

ANN: What? I just wanted to introduce myself while we're
stopped for a minute.

LISA: We're not stopped.

ANN: We seem to be in some sort of a pause here.

LISA: Because you're talking over the scene.

ANN: Oh, I'm sorry. Go on. I just wanted a quick hello. *(Confidentially, to Lisa)* It seems a little awkward to be going
along here without a little introduction, don't you think?

LISA *(Calculating that this will be the best way to deal with it)*: Okay. Go ahead. Quickly.

ANN *(Goes over to B, who plays Cynthia, and C, who plays Oscar)*: How're you doing?

LISA *(Reluctantly giving permission)*: It's okay. She just wants to say hi.

B AND C: Hi . . .

LISA: Okay, good—

ANN *(To Lisa)*: Well, what about the other two? We're all plopped out here together, we ought to say hello.

LISA *(Has no idea how to respond to this, then makes a snap decision to just do it and get it over with)*: D? A? A?! D?! I need you out here for a second.

(A and D, dressed for the upcoming Fourth of July scene, enter, thinking they must have missed their cue.)

ANN: Hi there.

(A and D are totally confused.)

LISA: No. It's not the scene. She just wants to say hi.

A AND D: Hi.

LISA *(Assuming they'll get back on track now)*: Okay, good, good. That's fine.

ANN: Are you all enjoying being in the play?

(The actors respond after a beat, not having really considered this question before.)

C: Yeah. It's nice.

B: It's okay . . .

A: Sure . . .

D *(Trying to be polite)*: It seems like an interesting story.

ANN: Oh? Which?

D: Oh. Uh . . . The neighborhood stuff?

ANN: Oh that part. Yeah, well, it was an incredible time. I wasn't sure for a minute which part. She's got a lot going on here.

A: Yeah, it's confusing.

C: It's a little confusing, yeah.

B: Yeah.

LISA: Well, it's not meant to be a "well-made play." It's a "theatrical exploration."

THE ACTORS: Um-hmm . . . Oh . . .

LISA: It's not a simple structure, I'll grant you that, but it's going to . . . come together. I was sick and then I got well . . . the neighborhood was sick and it got well . . .

(Uncomfortable pause.)

ANN: Would anybody like something to drink?

LISA: No, Mom, no. I'm doing a thing here.

(Lisa guides Ann back to her chair. The actors, with some confusion, assemble into the Fourth of July scene.)

This is where we look more closely at your use of social activities to build the political power of the Association.

ANN: Oh yeah. Everybody thought I was kooky about that, just like they think I'm kooky about the allergies now. Nobody could figure out why I'd put so much work into a Fourth of July celebration.

LISA: *That's* what I'm getting to. *(To the audience, commencing the next scene)* Social activities were the cornerstone of my mother's political methodology. In the beginning, as she says, people thought she was "kooky," but looking back it's clear my mother was actually a kind of housewife savant.

ANN *(To Lisa)*: Housewife savant!? That makes me sound like a halfwit. *(To the actors)* Don't you think?

(They shrug or nod, a little uncomfortable taking sides.)

LISA *(Continuing)*: The biggest of the social activities was a huge Fourth of July parade which ended in Saint Joe Park with a big potluck supper, prizes—

ANN *(To Lisa)*: You have to tell them about the carnival. *(To the audience)* There was a beanbag toss and—

LISA: Thank you, Mom. I was getting to that. *(Back to the audience)* There was a homemade carnival, and prizes were given out for best bike decoration and best float and best costume. The prize I most coveted was a three-foot-high doll with an elaborate antebellum-style dress made out of coffee filters by an elderly lady//who lived on Hillsdale—

ANN *(To the audience)*: Right. Althea Dickerson made those. They were beautiful! People were always telling me we should make it easier . . .

LISA *(Getting an idea)*: Mom!

ANN *(To Lisa)*: Oh, I'm sorry

LISA: No, you know what, Mom? Why don't you do this part?

ANN: What part?

LISA: This story. It's right where we are. You go ahead, Mom. It's your line.

ANN: What line? Oh, you mean like in the play? Oh, I don't think so. I don't want a line.

LISA: It's not a line. It's not a line. Just go ahead and say what you were already saying. Okay?

ANN: Well, okay. *(To the audience)* I was saying that people were always telling me that we should hire a midway, get gift certificates for prizes. But these old ladies would spend the whole year gathering costume jewelry and crocheting little purses and so forth to donate for the prizes, and it made them feel they had a stake in this neighborhood. Do you know what I mean? And so then when we'd suddenly get a phone call tipping us off that city council was going to push through some big zoning change we could get a hundred old ladies to show up at the meeting that afternoon. *(To the cast)* Okay now what did you want to drink?

LISA *(To Ann)*: No. Good, good, good. That's okay.

ANN *(To Lisa)*: Hey. Tell them about when you dressed up as the hamburger.

LISA: No.

(Slight pause.)

ANN *(Simultaneously with Lisa)*: Oh. Well then tell them about when you were the geisha.

LISA *(Simultaneously with Ann)*: I'm going to tell them about when I was the geisha.

(Both momentarily delighted by sharing the same idea.)

ANN *(Simultaneously with Lisa)*: That's just what I was going to tell you!

LISA *(Simultaneously with Ann)*: That's just what I was gonna do!

(Lisa continues to the audience. Ann resumes getting drink orders from the cast.)

Okay. One year I was a geisha. Pulling a ricksha—you know, the way geishas do. I wore a kimono she made me out of a plastic tablecloth that had a lovely Japanese pattern, and the added advantage of costing $1.79,//I'm sure—

ANN *(To Lisa)*: Oh, no, no. It wasn't that much.

LISA *(Continues, to the audience)*: The ricksha was made out of our garden cart. I was wrapped in plastic, basically, on the Fourth of July, and I pulled my ricksha valiantly until I reached the park, where I dropped in a dead faint. I remember her taking the costume off my sweaty little body,//exposing it to the air—

ANN *(Overcome with laughter; to the audience)*: Oh my god. I don't know what I was thinking! It was plastic!

LISA: I was wrapped in plastic on the Fourth of July.

ANN *(To Lisa)*: Oh, you looked awful cute. *(Hands Lisa the order sheet)* Okay, D wants a Coke, B and C both want Vernors, and A—boy, that name is just so different!— *(If any of the actors has an unusual name, it should be said last. Otherwise this aside should be cut)* wants lemon-lime seltzer, which I think you can find in the trunk of the car. *(Goes into her area to find her car keys)* You'll probably need to move some bags and boxes and stuff to get down to where it is. I bought a bunch of stuff at a rummage sale six months ago and I haven't had the strength to bring any of it in. *(Handing Lisa a huge ring of keys as she crosses to the actors)* I was always trying to find the human approach—

LISA: Mom?

ANN: Honey, just let me tell this story. *(Telling her story to the audience and the actors)* And I remember trying to get this realtor to sign one of our nondiscrimination pledges. And he was telling me how he couldn't in good conscience sign something like that because people really wanted to know if they were moving into a neighborhood where black people lived. They had strong feelings about it, you know. Well, I happened to know this guy was Catholic, and I said to him that I didn't have feelings one way or the other about black people because where I grew up there were none. But I did have a lot of bad feelings about Catholics, and I sure wished someone had told me before I bought this house that this neighborhood was just crawling with Catholics! *(To Lisa)* Oh, sorry, you were going to get the seltzer. What's the matter?

LISA: Nothing. It's just . . . *(Tearing up one of her note cards)* I was going to use that story later.

ANN: I keep forgetting. Oh, you've got a play to do. I'm so sorry, A, you go.

A: Really?//Okay. I don't know where I'm going.

LISA *(To Ann)*: No, no. I need her here. *(To the cast)* Okay. We're going to cut the end of this scene now//and go onto the next Allergy Unit scene.

(C and D exit to get ready for the next scene.)

B (*Pulling Lisa aside*): Lisa, could I ask you a quick question? (*A joins her*) Based on what we rehearsed—are we supposed to play these characters in the Unit as a little whacked? Or are we trying to convey that people actually got better? We're a little confused.

ANN: Absolutely people got better there. Lisa certainly did.

B: Really?

LISA (*Simultaneously with Ann*): Uh . . .

ANN (*Simultaneously with Lisa*): Oh my, yes. Oh, she was awful bad before she went. It was heartbreaking.

LISA (*To A and B*): Why don't you two just move through it the best you can right now?

ANN: When I had to drop out of college because I was so sick, you know, nobody knew anything about the allergies. One doctor told me I had mono six times.

B: Six times?

A: You're kidding!

(*Lisa forces A to go backstage.*)

LISA: B?

B: Hang on a second, honey. I'm talking to your mom.

ANN: And I said to him aren't you supposed to only be able to get it once, and he said, well, I don't know what to tell you but that's what you've got.

B: See, Lisa? This is so helpful.

LISA: It is. It's really helpful. Thank you so much, Mom. Come on, B.

ANN: Another doctor told me I had "Tired Housewives Syndrome." Now, the doctors who understand about allergy treat all sorts of things like depression and hyperactivity, vision problems . . .

B: Hyperactive? I have a nephew who's hyperactive.

ANN: That could be allergy.

B: Really?

ANN: Oh, absolutely. Hyperactivity is absolutely connected to sugar in kids. I have some copies here *(Goes to the overflowing shelves behind her chair and starts to pull a huge box down from the top shelf)* of some articles . . .

C *(Who has been setting up the next hospital scene)*: Do you need some help?

(B calls offstage to A and D, who have been backstage changing for their next hospital scene. A, C and D race over into Ann's area to help her with the box. They trip all over each other as Ann, oblivious, manages to plop the box down next to her chair, right where she wanted it. The actors, now in Ann's space for the first time, start to take it in.)

D: Wow, you're really organized back here.

ANN: Yeah, isn't that great? I built each section so that it would hold a specific thing. See? Wrapping paper? Thumbtacks? All kinds of tape? Here? See?

D: You built these?

ANN: Sure. My windup toy collection. All my stamps, all sorted by denomination? Isn't that cute? I just love it.

D: I can't believe you built these.

ANN: I built shelves and cupboards all through this house. Drives me crazy not to have enough storage *(Going through the box)* Now let's see.

C: Is this a candlesnuffer collection?

ANN: Where? Oh, yeah.

C: My mom collects candlesnuffers.

D: How did you get this detail?

ANN: Where?

D: Here.

ANN: Oh. I've got a router and a band saw in the basement.

(Lisa has now completed setting up the next Allergy Unit scene by herself.)

LISA: People, people, people, people, people PEOPLE! Please!

(The actors remember they're supposed to be in a play and return to their places for the next scene: Lisa and Joy are in their room with the Head Nurse.)

HEAD NURSE: You have made great progress in these past few days.

LISA: Really?

HEAD NURSE *(Checking his clipboard)*: Yeah. They switched you to the citrate of magnesia, didn't they? *(Lisa makes a face)* It's better than the milk of magnesia, isn't it?

LISA: Better?

HEAD NURSE: Yeah. A lot of people think it tastes like 7-UP.

LISA: I guess. If 7-UP were bottled by the devil and served in hell.

HEAD NURSE: You know what? You are ready to start food testing.

LISA: Really?

HEAD NURSE: Yeah. Joy? You're going to have a dining companion for your food test tonight.

LISA: So, starting now, couldn't I be done with food testing in time to get back to school before the end of the semester?

HEAD NURSE: It's possible. Depends how long it takes to find your safe foods.

JOY: Most people are here at least six weeks, but maybe you could get through sooner. The skin testing should work really well on you because you've got those big arms with a lot of surface area.

HEAD NURSE: Okay, Joy, should we go see how those beanbag filters work for you?

JOY: Yes.

(Joy exits with the Head Nurse.)

LISA *(Mocking Joy)*: "The skin testing should work really well on you because you've got those . . ."

(Lori Jones suddenly, shockingly, bangs in.)

LORI: Lisa Kron! Lisa!

(Lisa jumps. She turns and sees Lori.)

LISA: Oh shit!
LORI: Show us how you dance.
LISA: You know what? You're not in this. *(Pulling her note cards out of her pocket)* Look. See? *(Shows Lori her cards)* You're not in this. See?

(Lori swats the cards away and they scatter all over the floor.)

LORI: I don't care about those. Me and Belinda and Pam and Carol and Antoinette want to see you dance. Go on.
LISA *(Stevie Wonder's "Superstition" begins to play and Lisa is suddenly catapulted into a memory; to the audience)*: Third grade. Nine years old. The teacher has left the room. Oh, I hate when that happens. Somebody's put their own record on the school record player. What is this song? "Very Superstitious"? Why have I never heard this song before? How come everybody else knows this song? This is exactly like when I go to Young Judea conventions and all of the other girls show up wearing black Chinese slippers or painter pants. HOW ARE THESE PEOPLE COMMUNICATING WITH EACH OTHER??

(Lori menaces her.)

(To herself) Wait, no, look bored, look bored. Act like you don't care. Do not let Lori see you with your guard down—
LORI: I said show us how you dance. Are you deaf?
LISA: No. And I'm not nine years old!
LORI: You're not dancing, either. You gonna dance?
LISA *(Humiliated)*: No.
LORI: Um-hmm. *(To the audience)* See? What'd I tell you.

(Lori turns on her heel and exits. Lisa stands stunned for a moment, then she begins to gather her scattered cards.

Nurse 2 and Joy enter. They are momentarily taken aback to see Lisa picking up the cards, but they continue to play their scene.)

NURSE 2: Lisa, you have a food test.

LISA *(Gathering herself, and reassuring the actors that she's with them)*: Right! Mmm. My first food test. Thank you.

NURSE 2 *(Handing Lisa her tray)*: For you, madam, corn.

LISA: Thank you.

NURSE 2 *(Handing Joy her tray)*: And Joy.

JOY: Thank you.

(Nurse 2 exits.)

(Takes her pulse. Speaking internally as she writes in her book) Starting pulse: sixty-six. Baseline: plus-one level irritability.

(Lisa sits on her bed.)

LISA *(Takes her pulse. Speaking internally as she writes in her book)*: Starting pulse: sixty-eight. Baseline symptoms: don't know, feel pretty good.

(They eat.)

What are you testing, Joy?

JOY: Pineapple.

LISA: That sounds good. Is it good?

JOY: It's fine. So far.

(They eat.)

LISA: Hmm! Oh my god. This corn is delicious! Is this so good because it's organic or because I haven't eaten anything in six days?

(They keep eating.)

This is so good!

JOY: You know, if you really love a food, chances are you're allergic to it.

LISA: Is that right?

JOY: Yes, well, obviously. If you love it and feel like you can't live
without it, or if you can't stand the thought of it, that
probably means you're allergic. Oh. Ten minutes.

(Each takes her pulse and records it again in her notebook.)

LISA *(Speaking internally)*: Pulse: sixty-eight. Still feel okay.

JOY *(Speaking internally)*: Pulse: seventy-five. Plus-two level
irritability.

LISA: You know, I think I might be okay with corn. I don't feel
anything different so far.

JOY: Well, that would be really lucky for you. You'd be one of the
very rare people who doesn't react to it. Corn! Corn is in
everything. Corn syrup, corn . . . all kinds of corn. In everything. But, you know, if you're having a reaction or not, the
accuracy of this testing is completely up to you. No doctor is going to hold your hand. It's all about honest self-
assessment of your reactions. Oh. Twenty minutes.

(They write again.)

LISA *(Speaking internally)*: Pulse: sixty-eight still. Paranoia? No,
Joy is picking on me. I'm fine.

JOY *(Speaking internally)*: Pulse: seventy-nine. Intense feelings
of aggression toward roommate. Can't control it. Plus-
three . . . *(To Lisa)* You know, Lisa, I hope you're not wor-
rying about gaining back the weight you lost during your
fast. *(Speaking internally)* . . . and a half. *(Buzzes the nurses
station)* Can you send a nurse in here, please? I think I need
to be neutralized.

(Ann makes a horrible noise of pain. Lisa and A drop the scene and turn to look. Lisa glares at Ann.)

ANN *(Still gasping in pain)*: Oy boy. Oy boy.

LISA *(To Ann)*: Are you all right?

ANN: Yeah.

A *(To Lisa)*: Is she okay?

ANN: I'm fine. *(Another yelp)* Oh, I don't know, when I move in a certain way it's just like I'm being stabbed with a poker!

A *(To Ann)*: Do you need a pillow or something?

LISA: No. She said she's fine.

ANN: Yeah. I'm about to take a pain pill *(Reaches for her glass; more pain)* Oh! If I could reach that glass of water. It's just a little out of my reach unless I get up out of this chair, which I would rather not do right now.

(A jumps up and gets the glass for Ann.)

A: Are you sure you're all right?

ANN: Yeah, I'll be fine. *(A heads back to resume the scene)* Listen, when you get a chance would you give this to B? I think she might find this interesting too.

A: Okay. What is it?

ANN: Oh, it's about formaldehyde exposure in stores. You know, a lot of people get real sick when they go to a mall, terrible headaches, and so forth.

A: No kidding.

ANN: Oh yeah. They don't realize it's the formaldehyde fumes in all the merchandise. They get disoriented and cranky and sometimes they get numbness in their limbs.

A: That happens to me.

ANN: It's probably allergy.

A: I just thought it was some spiritual response to consumerist culture.

ANN: No, it's probably the formaldehyde.

A: Really? That is unbelievable. Do you have a copy I could . . . ?

WELL

ANN: Sure.

A *(Reading the article)*: "Nausea . . . headaches . . . disorientation . . ." This is exactly what happens to me every time I go into a mall. My friends are like, you're such a drag, A, get it together. I can't believe this. I have always assumed it was just me.

ANN: Well, yeah, that's what happens. You blame yourself. Wasn't it Susan Sontag who pointed out that whenever the cause of an illness is mysterious, it's assumed to come from psychological problems or a moral weakness. And once science finally figures out the medical root of the illness, that assumption disappears. That's why it's so important that more people know about the allergies.

A: I feel so relieved.

ANN: I know.

(Lisa, who has been watching this exchange, quietly channels her fury into a polite request.)

LISA: Hey, A?

(Lisa picks up both food testing trays and takes them offstage.)

A: I have to go. I like talking to you better though.

ANN: Aw, now. She's more used to the one-woman shows. She's figuring it out.

A: Okay. See you later.

ANN: Okay. A? A? *(Gets her attention)* Would you give this to her? *(Gives A an old, worn piece of paper that she discovered in a box earlier)*

(Tiniest pause.)

A *(To Ann, confirming)*: Lisa?

ANN: Yes. I just found it. It's really interesting.

A: Okay.

(A returns to the Unit setting. Lisa returns from offstage.)

LISA *(With thinly veiled sarcasm and anger)*: Oh, great, you're back! We're going to do the other testing scene now. The later one? Where you enter?

A: Oh. Okay.

(A is flushed. She hands Lisa the paper. Lisa stares at it for one second, perplexed, and then stuffs it into her pocket. She gestures impatiently to A to start the scene. A exits and enters again as Joy. She's very shaken. Lisa's anger over A's betrayal and A's vulnerability from the quiet catharsis she's just had with Ann, color the way they play this scene with each other.)

LISA: Joy, where have you been?

JOY: I was chem testing today.

LISA: Yeah, but they took you away hours ago. Have you just been in the chem test room all this time sniffing little bottles of—what were you testing today?

JOY: Formaldehyde.

(Tiny pause as they both realize A's mistake.)

LISA: Don't you mean phenol?

JOY: Oh, right. Phenol.

LISA: Right. Have you just been in the chem test room all this time sniffing little bottles of phenol?

JOY: No.

LISA: Oh. Well, you missed it here. I tested yeast.

JOY: How did you do?

LISA: Oh, my god, Joy—it was a nightmare. Well, I didn't realize they were just going to give me my pitcher of cold water and my pitcher of hot water and a packet of yeast. How was I supposed to know what to do with that, you know? So I thought, Well, it'll be better with the hot water.

JOY: That's not a good idea.

LISA: Yeah, well, I know that now! Oh god, Joy, it frothed-up out of control. And you know what I did? I lapped it up. Like a dog. Like a yeast-eating dog. You know what, Joy? Never mind. You want to be miserable? Be miserable.

(D, entering as the Head Nurse, can feel quickly that something bad has transpired between Lisa and A.)

HEAD NURSE: Joy, how are you feeling?
JOY: Okay.
HEAD NURSE: Okay, no more testing tonight.
LISA *(To Head Nurse)*: What happened?
HEAD NURSE: Joy had an extreme reaction to the phenol and went into anaphylactic shock. They almost had to take her down to intensive care. *(Pointedly)* You should try to keep the conversation to a minimum. Okay?

(The Head Nurse exits.)

LISA *(Trying to really apologize)*: Joy, I'm sorry.
JOY *(A's personal vulnerability is clearly coming through)*: I know I'm no fun. I know I'm hard to be around. It's not what I want. I'm just so tired of being sick.

(Lisa is totally taken aback. She gathers herself and attempts to begin the next scene. A starts to exit, then suddenly veers back toward Lisa.)

LISA: Oscar's father, Mr. Harris is my mother's . . .
A *(Grabbing Lisa's arm)*: Lisa, this is intense.

(A exits. Lisa is rendered speechless.)

ANN *(To Lisa)*: Everything okay?
LISA *(Defensive)*: Yes. *(Suddenly)* Mom, this next scene is about when you went over and talked to Mr. Harris that time when and he and Mrs. Harris had that fight . . .

ANN: Oh, I remember that—

LISA *(Cutting her off)*: I know you do, and I just want you to know that we've got the whole scene all planned out.

ANN: Okay.

(Big Oscar enters along with the neighborhood setting.)

LISA: Oscar's father, Mr. Harris, is my mother's friend.

BIG OSCAR: Ann Kron!

LISA: During the week our parents talk for hours over the fence that separates our backyards, chatting about the neighborhood, the news, their kids . . . On the weekends, though, Mr. Harris drinks.

BIG OSCAR: Ann Kron! Did you hear me?

LISA: Only on the weekends, and only beer, but it's enough to get him going. And that's when he pokes at this friendly relationship with the whites next door. It seems like he's trying to see whether, if he pokes hard enough to puncture the surface, the racist bile will seep out. And that's when he stands on our front walk and yells:

BIG OSCAR: Hey, Ann. Come on out here and give me a kiss!

LISA: Sometimes my mother ignores him. Sometimes she opens the door and says, "Oh Oscar, go home." Sometimes he comes in the house and makes pronouncements to me and my brother—gets close in our faces and bathes us in beery breath and says:

BIG OSCAR *(With total drunken gravitas)*: Your father is a lawyer.

LISA: And we panic because it's not at all clear what the polite response to this might be. Many times he says to my mother:

BIG OSCAR: Ann Kron, if I'd married you, I'd be a happy man today.

LISA: And she always responds, "Oscar, if you'd married me, you'd be a dead man, because I'd never put up with you the way Rosalie does." But one Sunday in the late afternoon, Little Oscar's parents were fighting. And suddenly we heard Little Oscar screaming. And my mother charged out the door.

(A and D enter as Dottie and Howard.)

My father and some other neighbors were standing at the end of the Harris's front walk and she said, "Did you hear that? What are we going to do?" And they said:

DOTTIE: I don't know.

HOWARD: What can we do?

LISA: And she said, "I heard that child scream and I'm going to find out what's going on." And she walked up the walk and knocked on the door. And Mr. Harris opened the door and he said:

BIG OSCAR: Ann, stay out of this. This is colored people's business.

LISA: She said, "Oscar? You speak for yourself, but don't you dare drag a whole race of people down with you. Now move. I'm going to go see if that child is all right." And she pushed him aside and went upstairs and took Little Oscar by the hand and brought him to our house for the evening. And Mr. Harris, he let her, of course, because he and my mother were neighbors. They were friends—

(Lori smashes into the scene, scaring the crap out of Lisa, and bewildering A, C and D, who don't know who this little girl is or why Lisa's so afraid of her.)

LORI: Lisa!

LISA: What do you want?!

LORI: What do you have to do with your hair? *(Pokes Lisa in the head)*

LISA: What do you mean?

LORI: How do you take care of your hair?

LISA *(Trying to play it off)*: Uh, I wash it and I brush it.

LORI: See? What'd I tell you? *(Pulling at Lisa's hair)* Ugly, stringy, nasty. Eew.

LISA *(Doing her best to be firm)*: Okay. I'm going to have to ask you to leave—

LORI: You're gonna what? *(A threatening pause)* You're gonna what?

(Lisa is trapped in Lori's treacherous gaze for a moment, until suddenly Lori makes a move and chases Lisa across the stage into Ann's area, where she is now cornered.)

ANN: What's going on?

LISA: I don't know!! I'm being tormented by a nine year old from my past, who is creating a totally wrong impression about the neighborhood. *(To the audience)* What I am trying to convey is that the Association stabilized the neighborhood and, by the way, it's still a stable racially integrated neighborhood today in 2006 when most people don't even remember when that was a goal! Okay, there might have been a little bit of tension between some of the kids. But the big picture is that the Neighborhood Association was working. The adults were getting along.

ANN: What are you talking about? Of course there was tension among the adults.

LORI *(Having proven her point)*: HA!

(Lori exits triumphantly.)

ANN: Well, you know that, honey. You're right, the Association was very successful—

LISA: Yes!

ANN: . . . but there were certainly tensions. Howard and Jim, for instance, you remember that whole thing?

LISA: Yes,//I remember Howard and—

ANN *(Continuing over Lisa, to C and D)*: You two were supposed to be Howard and Jim, right?

C AND D: Yeah, right.

ANN: Now, see, you've got those two looking all helpful and engaged, but I'll tell you, those two were condescending as all get out.

D: Really?

ANN: Yes. Well, you know, they took over.

C: Took over?

ANN: Oh, did she not tell you that?

C, D AND A: No.

LISA *(Muttering to herself)*: Okay, go ahead. Tell the story.

ANN: Oh yeah. At the end of the second year, when it was suddenly clear that the Association had become a major political power in the city of Lansing, Jim ran against me for president because, as he said: "Now that the Association has gotten some power it's time for a man to take over."

C, D AND A *(Uproar)*: No way! . . . You're kidding! . . .

(Ann gestures for the cast to come closer and they gather around her chair. As she tells this story, Lisa, totally frustrated, attempts to complete the next scene change on her own.)

ANN: Oh yes. Well those two were convinced from the beginning that I didn't know what I was doing. And when Jim took over, they went ahead and cut all the things that they thought were so frivolous—the door-to-door newsletter delivery and the holiday decorating and all of that—and at the end of the year all the power was gone and no one was even showing up for meetings.

C: Wait a minute, Jim won?

ANN: Oh yeah. Well, I told people to vote for him.

A: Why?

ANN: I sure didn't like how condescending they were, but frankly I was relieved that someone else was finally willing to take over. I hadn't been well enough to do it in the first place.

D: But I thought you were president for more than two years?

ANN: Oh, I was overwhelmingly reelected the next year. Everybody missed the Fourth of July.

C: Okay, now, Lisa, this would have been a good scene!

ANN: Well sure. See now, Lisa, this is what I was concerned about in the beginning, when you had that scene that was so oversimplified—you can't really take years of complicated political work and compress it down into a two-minute—

A, C AND D: Montage.

ANN: Right. You just can't boil it down like that. It was all so complicated and interesting. But I'll tell you something about that election—it was incredible, and even Jim said it at the time—that though there was divisiveness it never fell along racial lines.

LISA *(Reinserting herself)*: Right. That's the point that I was trying to make!

ANN: What point, honey? It's true you had some tension with some of the black kids, but, honey, you didn't fit in particularly well with the white kids either. You were your own person—which is one of the things I really like about you. Did you tell them how unusual you were?

LISA: Yeah, I think I mentioned it.

ANN *(To the cast)*: Did she tell you about how she used to dress up in interesting costumes?

(The entire cast hunkers down for a good story.)

D: No. Uh-uh.

ANN: Honey, tell that story.

LISA: No.

ANN: Why not? *(To the cast)* It's very entertaining.

C: We'd love to hear that.

A *(Overlapping C)*: We'd love it.

LISA: Okay, that's enough.

D: So she didn't have any friends?

LISA: I had friends. Mom?

ANN: She had a couple of friends.

LISA: Okay—

A: So the story . . . ?

LISA: Hey. Hey. Hey. Hey. Hey. Okay, chit-chat hour is over. I need you in place, now, for the next scene.

D: What is the next scene?

A: Yeah. We don't know where we are.

(A pause. For a moment Lisa doesn't know where they are either.)

ANN: While she figures it out, just let me tell you quickly about these parties—

A: Oh goody.

LISA: No! No! We're moving on!

ANN *(Continuing from above; to the audience)*: Lisa should really be telling you this story because she remembers all kinds of details I can't keep track of, but one year she dressed up as a—oh, Lisa, how does this go? You remember it better.

(Overlapping Ann, Lisa gets the cast up and pushes them off-stage, instructing them to get ready for the next Allergy Unit scene, and they tell her they have costume changes and set pieces to think about, and they can't just appear in a new scene. Lisa pushes them off, telling them to go and work it out. The actors exit.)

LISA *(To Ann)*: Mom, please. Shh.

(A pause while Lisa looks expectantly offstage, waiting for the actors to reappear ready for the next scene—but, nothing.)

(To the audience) Okay, so every year I would get invited to Susie's Halloween party.

ANN: Oh good! I love this story.

LISA: And every year I would think and think about my costume, believing, as I did, because my mother told me that it was so, that there was nothing more important or valuable than originality and creativity. And the first year I went to this party, after a great deal of thought, I decided that I would go as the Little Match Girl—which doesn't sound all that original, I know, but I decided to do it *authentic*. And so I found these nasty clothes in the basement somewhere and ratted my hair really bad, and there was dirt, like, I rubbed real dirt all over myself. And the result was, I have to say, excellent. And I could not wait to get to this party and walk in and be like: "This is it, girls, this is what real creativity looks like." And I got to this party, and I walked in, and I saw that all the other little girls, every one, was dressed as a beautiful princess. And I thought: Okay. This is not going to work out the way I pictured it. You're all princesses and I'm clever, sort of, but not really, because I'm covered in dirt.

And then we spent the rest of the day playing this game called "Fairies," which is a game in which you go outside and run around the perimeter of the yard pretending to be a fairy. And the fun of this game, if you happen to be dressed as a princess, is you feel the breeze blowing through your pretty hair and you can feel your pretty dress fluttering behind you and you feel really pretty. That's the point. And I played along because—what else was I going to do? I had actually chosen ugliness. For some reason I couldn't remember anymore, I had actually chosen ugliness and now I had to clomp around in it surrounded by fluttering beauties. I thought to myself—and not for the first time— Adulthood must surely be better than this. And I vowed that the next year I would also be a princess.

And the next year came. And I did remember my vow, but, again, I got swept up again in thinking about how fantastic it would be to do something original and creative. And I came up with what I thought would be a really, really, good idea. I would be a princess, but I would be The Princess of Five—who was the princess of everything five. She would wear five layers of clothing. She'd wear five watches—all set to five o'clock. She'd have five braids in her hair. Etcetera. And on my way to the party I was so excited! Because—come on! And I got there. And I walked in. And there they were—all the pretty girls in their pretty dresses, and I thought, What is wrong with me?! What in the world is wrong with me??

And again, we were going to spend four hours playing the "Look at What a Pretty Princess I Am" game, flappy-flapping the pretty fairy wings—and I had plenty to flap because there was five of everything.

And I was stuck. Stuck, stuck, stuck.

(Pause. Still no cast members.)

I *did* have two friends, by the way. Beth and Ann, who shared my desire to be original and creative. We met in the fifth grade when the Neighborhood Association instituted a voluntary busing program—this was before the court mandated busing—and this program brought a few more white kids, besides me and my brother, into Main Street School. The three of us hit it off immediately, partly, probably, because we were all the daughters of progressive whites, but, more to the point, I think, probably, because of our shared obsession with Laura Ingalls Wilder. And I mean "obsession." The three of us read and reread and discussed all of her books. And at some point we realized we could take our love for our idol to the next level and actually dress like her. And at that point, we got our mothers to sew us prairie dresses. Authentic. Just like Laura's. Made out of calico. And, of course, with sunbonnets.

ANN *(To the audience)*: They could not have been more adorable.

LISA: When they were finished we met at Beth's house. We spent an incredible day in her backyard driving our teams of oxen and fighting back prairie fires. And it was so incredible, that when it was time to go home, we made a pact with each other that the next day all three of us would wear these dresses—to school.

I remember that day, actually. I remember walking up the wide sidewalk to the school door, starting to feel a little queasy. I remember how, entering the hall a voice in my head began to scream, MISTAKE! MISTAKE! MISTAKE!

One of the most horrible things about being a child, the primary thing that made me think every day, I can't wait to be an adult, and that has made me grateful every day of my adult life that I am no longer a child, is that, as an adult, you can just leave. But on that day there was no taking back that I had walked into my fifth grade class at Main Street School dressed like Laura Ingalls Wilder.

(Lori Jones enters, looks at Lisa, and bursts into loud, derisive laughter.)

(To the audience) Okay I would like to make something clear here. I would like you to know that Lori Jones is not representative of my experience growing up in this neighborhood.

LORI: Kronberger. You're a Kronberger. You know that? *(Poking Lisa on each syllable)* Kron. Ber. Ger.

LISA *(To the audience)*: The thing that Lori Jones' presence here does not make clear is that—

(Lori moves in on Lisa and runs her finger up Lisa's back.)

LORI *(Overlapping)*: How come you ain't got no bra on yet?
LISA *(Overlapping)*: —it does not make clear that growing up—
LORI *(Overlapping)*: Hmm? How come you don't answer me?
LISA *(Overlapping)*: —growing up in this neighborhood was a positive—
LORI *(Overlapping)*: Are you deaf?
LISA *(Overlapping)*: —it was a positive experience, but Lori J—
LORI *(Overlapping)*: I said: "Are You Deaf?" Huh? Huh? Huh?

LISA *(Overlapping)*: —Lori Jones is not helping to establish that. Seeing her is just going to play into any stereotypes you might already be holding.

(Lisa suddenly attempts to fight back. A lame girl-fight ensues in which Lisa falls and Lori tries to drag her offstage.)

I can't believe I'm getting beat up in my own play! This is *absurd.*

(Ann gets up and grabs Lori by the arm and pulls her off Lisa.)

ANN *(To Lori)*: All right, missy. Cut that out. Shame on you. Cut that out. *(Holds Lori by the arm)*

LORI *(To Lisa)*: I don't care if you don't want me in your stupid play. What're you going to do about it? 'Cause I was in your stupid life.

ANN: All right then. You scoot. I know for a fact your mother doesn't approve of this kind of rudeness. Scoot.

LORI *(Chastised)*: Yes, ma'am.

(Lori starts to exit. She glares at the audience.)

What are you looking at? Stupid white girl. Stupid girl acts like she's scared of me so I give her something to be scared of.

(Lori exits.)

LISA: Do you see why I don't want her in my . . . pl—exploration???

ANN: Well, yes and no. Bad manners is one thing. I used to kick kids out of the yard for bad manners, regardless of whether they were black or white. So that's one thing. Kick Lori out of the play for acting like a crumb if you want, but not because she's not an appropriate "representation."

Part of the point of growing up in an integrated neighbor-hood was that you didn't have to extrapolate from abstract impressions of black people, because you knew actual people. Lori didn't have that kind of power. She was just one little girl.

(Beat.)

LISA: I know that. That's not what my issue—that's not my issue. Look, it's fine. Okay? It's really fine. My only thing is that I just want to be able to do the play—
ANN: Exploration.
LISA: Exploration, okay, exploration without interruption. Okay?
ANN: Yes.
LISA: Okay. Good. Good. Good. Good. Good. Good. That's what we're gonna do then.

(Lisa crosses to complete the unfinished scene change to the Allergy Unit.)

ANN *(Following her)*: Okay. But first, I need to correct something.

(Heavy, irritated sigh from Lisa.)

I didn't bring Little Otis//back here . . .
LISA *(Trying to cover her mother's mistake)*: Oscar.
ANN: What?
LISA: Oscar.
ANN: Oh right, Oscar, I guess you're calling him here. I didn't bring him back here that night. He was here plenty of other times, but not that night. I stayed with him until his father calmed down. He didn't come over here.
LISA: Yes he did.
ANN: No he didn't.
LISA: That's the way I've always heard the story.

ANN: I don't know from whom. The rest of it was right, but that last part—I think you must have made that up so you could have a nice ending. It's just that I've noticed a number of little inaccuracies as you've been going along.

(As Ann continues, Lisa goes offstage and gets B, who enters dressed as Kay. She is rattled by the shuffled order of the scenes and by Lisa's angry energy toward her mom, for whom B now has very affectionate feelings.)

I find it curious that you never show yourself having a reaction. It's almost like you're trying to make it seem like you weren't really sick in the hospital. Honey, turn out. You've got your back to the audience. Is that the impression you mean to give?

LISA: Mom, we are so off track!!!

ANN: I'm sorry.

LISA: No, I'm sorry. I don't mean to yell. Would you sit down? Do you need anything?

ANN *(Sitting in her chair)*: No.

LISA: Okay, I need to finish the scene.

ANN: Okay.

(Lisa crosses back to enter the next Unit scene. Kay is packing.)

LISA: Hi, Kay.

KAY: Hello.

LISA: Is your cousin coming to pick you up?

KAY: No. My sister.

LISA: That's good.

KAY: Yeah, I guess it's good.

LISA: No?

(Kay slams something down on the bed.)

Do you think you're having a reaction?

KAY: I don't know. Maybe. I guess.

LISA: Do you want me to go get you some alkali salts?

KAY: No. Lisa . . . It's not fair. I don't want to be sick. My sister is cleaning my house for me, getting my safe room ready. She is good to me, but I can't help it. I don't want her going through my things. Oh, I don't know, I don't know. I'm not reacting. I'm ANGRY. I'm SO ANGRY, LISA. I know she thinks if she were me she'd be better, but do you know what the problem is with being sick? It's that you're sick. People who are healthy think they know how you could get better, because when they imagine what your life is like they imagine having your sickness on top of their health. They imagine that sick people have all the resources they do and they're just not trying hard enough. But we don't. I don't. I know my sister is only trying to help me, but I can't help it. I think, You suffer for just one day the way I do. I want you to feel like this for just one day. Then you tell me how to get better.

(Lisa, dislocated by a memory that has overcome her, steps into her special light. Kay exits.)

LISA: My mother's always been sick, but when I was sixteen she almost died. I'm sorry—why am I just remembering this? She almost died and we didn't notice. I know, right? But she was always sick, you know. So when one day she couldn't climb the stairs without passing out, we didn't think that much about it; we just brought a mattress downstairs and put it in the middle of the living room floor. I know, it's terrible. She had this racking cough, I remember. It drove me crazy—I couldn't hear the TV, you know. About a week later—I think—she said to my dad, "You have to take me to the emergency room." And, of course, they admitted her right away. And a few days later the doctors apparently told my dad he better make arrangements for his children because his wife was probably going

W
E
L
L

59

to die. And we still didn't get it. I remember I'd drive myself up to the hospital every day after school and just sit with her, watch her gasping for breath, barely conscious.

(A new layer is suddenly remembered) But one day when I went in, she was sitting up. She was better. Steroids. They'd pumped her full of steroids. And within hours she was better. And the whole time she was on the steroids, which I think was for months after, she was healthy. She was the healthiest she ever was in her whole life.

(Shaking it off) She couldn't stay on them of course. You can't stay on steroids indefinitely. So then she got sick again.

(Lisa steps out of the light and heads back to finish the Allergy Unit scene change.)

ANN: Lisa?

LISA: What?

ANN: I want to make sure you're going to have a scene about your wheat reaction. *(To the audience)* She had an awful big wheat reaction when she was in the hospital. *(To Lisa)* Do you remember how you were just crying and crying until they neutralized you?

LISA *(Continuing with the scene change, holding her temper in a vise-grip of control)*: Yeah, I remember it.

ANN: Oh. Okay. I was starting to get afraid you weren't going to tell that part of the story.

(Lisa continues with the scene change, she doesn't respond.)

Are you telling that part of the story?

LISA *(As evenly as she can possibly manage)*: Mom, the thing is, this is not about me. And it's not about you. This a theatrical construct.

ANN: Well, whatever it is, I don't see how they're going to understand how you learned to cope with the allergies if you don't tell them about what happened to you while you were in the Unit.

LISA: Well, I really have given some thought to what I'm doing here—

ANN: Well I would assume so, but so far I haven't seen any parts where you get any help in the Unit. You had the wheat reaction;//you found out about your candida problem—

LISA: I HAD A WHEAT REACTION. I HAD A BIG WHEAT REACTION! IT'S NOT THE POINT!

ANN: What in the world is going on with you!?

LISA: NOTHING'S GOING ON WITH ME! I'M FINE! YOU KNOW WHAT? WHY DON'T YOU DO YOUR OWN SHOW? YOU HAVE A CLEAR IDEA ABOUT WHAT'S REALLY SUPPOSED TO BE GOING ON HERE, SO GO AHEAD. YOU TELL THEM THE "REAL STORY," SINCE APPARENTLY I'M NOT DOING IT RIGHT. I'LL GO UPSTAIRS. I'LL READ THIS MAGAZINE ... WHICH I'M *TOTALLY* INTERESTED IN. HAVE A REALLY FUN TIME, MOM, BECAUSE IT'S YOUR SHOW!

(Lisa grabs a magazine and stomps up the stairs. She sits at the top, pretending to be occupied reading.)

ANN: I don't want a show. I just want to watch my tapes.

(To the audience) She must be having a reaction. There's a storm front coming in, and I think everyone's affected by it. *(Pause; to Lisa)* Lisa? Your audience is still here, honey. You ought to come back down.

(Back to the audience) Oh lord. Okay, well ... Do you follow the ice-skating? I just love it. I watch it and doze for a little while, then I rewind and watch some more—I apologize for Lisa. You all didn't pay to get in here did you? Oh, this is terrible.

So ... let's see ... As you might have gathered, I don't really enjoy being on display in front of a group. Although I must say I did do a lot of it when I was doing the Association, and it's funny to me because I've really been a very insecure person most of my life, but there was something about that work that I felt so sure about. I don't know where I got my ideas about integration and so forth, because the town where I grew up was all white, so it's not like I had any personal experience with it. But I had such strong ideas about it from a very young age, and I cannot tell you where they came from. I did read things, I suppose. And then I went to Antioch. And part of that was because they were one of only two schools in the Midwest then that accepted blacks. But a big part of it, frankly, was because they also didn't have intramural sports and I was just so turned off by the whole sports thing. And so I went to Antioch, and the summer after my freshman year I went to live with my roommate, Quandra's family in Baltimore, which, at that time, 1952 . . . '53 . . . (I can never remember dates), was still segregated, of course. And living with a black family in segregated Baltimore, well, that just changed my life.

I guess when I went there I had very strong feelings about the evils of segregation and the evils of discrimination and all that. I had all the emotional reactions to it but none of the real life, practical information about it. But when I went out and applied for jobs . . . well, I still clearly remember sitting there, talking to an employer. They're just open and friendly and just as, you know, and clearly they're going to hire me. It isn't a question. I know I'm hired. And once I put that address down and they see it's in a black neighborhood—I can feel—it was very subtle, they weren't mean or angry—but I felt that all the sudden the door was closed. You know, I think before I went to Baltimore I somehow pictured that being black was just like being white only you were also black. Isn't that funny? But through that experience of living there I started to realize that you just don't imagine anyone else's situation is very different from yours unless you've been in a situation where you're different yourself. And I think that was an amazing thing for a white girl who'd never had any experience outside her own world.

Those years I did the Neighborhood Association—it was so hard. Every day. That kind of fatigue—not fatigue—there should be another word. It's like some kind of irresistible voice calling you all day to just close your eyes. Just give in and close your eyes. And I worked so hard, I had to work so hard to fight it. Even when I was sleeping, I was dreaming that I was trying to stay awake. But what kept me going those years, was that I kept thinking, When I die I don't want it to say on my gravestone: "She kept a clean house."

I haven't done so much in the last twenty years. There's so much I would do if I had the energy. You can't imagine. Sometimes I feel like the work I did in the neighborhood, that . . . it expired or something. I keep thinking, sitting here, That maybe now it's going to say on my gravestone: "She kept a dirty house."

Lisa was a quiet child—hard to imagine now, I know. She just sat and watched everything. She is like an amazing star to me—my daughter. But I . . . I don't even know how to say it. It's like we were one thing. Or we were rooted in the same place and she kept growing which was the most wonderful thing. To see her branch off and to have a life so different, and to have all that energy that I couldn't even imagine. But I guess I never questioned that we were starting from the same place. But I think maybe she doesn't feel that.

(Ann waits for a response from Lisa. There is none. She retreats into her private thoughts, and then transitions into an emotionally exhausted half-sleeping state. There is dead air onstage. Then a hushed, panicked discussion can be heard backstage:)

D: What's happening out there?!

A: I don't know. What *is* this?

C: Oh, I'll tell you what it is. It's some kind of fucked-up downtown bullshit.

D: Whose idea was it to put this bullshit on Broadway!

A: It's so fucked-up. It's so intense. I feel like I'm going to pass out.

D: It's hideous.

A: Should we try to . . . pick it up somewhere?

B: You're kidding, right?

C: Where?

A: I don't know. How about one of the parts where her mother saves the neighborhood?

B: Yeah, well, I don't know. I mean, I love Ann but the white woman saving all the black people? I don't think so.

A: I don't think that's what she's trying to say.

B: No. You wouldn't.

C: What are we going to do?

A: I don't know but someone's got to rescue Ann.

D: Who?

A, B AND C *(To D)*: You! Yeah, you. You do it. Go, go, go.

(D gets pushed onstage by the others.)

D *(To the audience)*: We apologize for this. We don't really have anything to do with it. We were just hired to be in it. *(Uncomfortable pause)* Thank you. *(Escapes back offstage with the other actors)*

B: What was that?

D: I'm sorry, you guys, I freaked-out. I don't know what to do.

(The following lines are jumbled together.)

B: That was bullshit.

D: I'm sorry. I freaked-out out there.

A: What are we going to do?

C: Should we leave?

D: Can we do that?

A: Can we just leave?

(At the threat of their leaving, Lisa races down the stairs to reengage them. The actors' next lines overlap, and all are cut off as soon as Lisa reaches them and gets their attention.)

c: Who's Equity deputy?

B: You.

c: Fuck. I don't know what to do.

D: It's hideous.

B: If you say that word one more time I swear . . .

D: Please hit me and put me out of my misery.

c: I need these weeks for my health insurance. Fuck. Fuck. Fuck. Fuck. Fuck.

A: What's going to happen to Ann?—

LISA (Attempting to pick up as if nothing's gone wrong): Okay, guys. Hey, you guys? Sorry we got a little bit off track. We're going to go to scene 12. So if you want to get into place for that.

(Nobody moves.)

Okay? Scene 12? Could we get in place for that?

(The actors reluctantly follow Lisa into the playing area.)

c: Lisa, wait.

LISA: What?

B: What are you doing?

LISA: We're going to pick it up. Scene 12.

A: Lisa, this is—

LISA: What?

A: I don't—I don't think we can just go on. You just left your mother stranded//out there—

B (*Overlapping a bit*): Yes, this is very uncomfortable.

LISA: Guys, I know this hasn't worked out the way I said that it would. I get that. I understand things got off track. I will deal with it. I promise. I will take care of her. After we do this scene.

A: I can't.

LISA: Yes, you can.

A: No, I can't. I know this sounds crazy, but I'm in love with your mother.

LISA: What?

A: I just feel so seen by her. So accepted. In such a deep way. So— I don't know. This doesn't feel okay anymore. I think your setup here is . . . well? . . . Manipulative and *wrong*.

D: Confused at best.

B: Yeah, I think that's how we all feel.

LISA: Okay. Well, I don't know what to say. She's not your mother, A. And I get all that stuff you're saying about her—I feel it, too. But I also live with the other stuff. Sometimes I see her in that almost comatose state in that chair—even just to raise her arm a little or turn her head makes her gasp in pain, and I get angry. She can't walk. She can't move. The moaning—the moaning drives me CRAZY. Does it not drive you crazy? What is the difference between that body and mine? What thin membrane separates us, really? I look at her in that state and I feel like I'm going to drown!

(*Pause.*)

B: Lisa, you have got a lot of intense shit going on with your mother.

LISA: No.

A: Lisa, I think you need to talk with your mother about these feelings.

LISA: No!

A: Why not?

LISA: Because she couldn't handle it. Because—how did we get on this topic? Since when do we get to have a conversation in the middle of a play?

B *(Suddenly deciding)*: You know what, Lisa? We're going to go.

LISA: No.

B: Yes, I think we need to leave now.

LISA: No.

B: Come on you guys. Lets say good-bye to Ann.

LISA: No. You can't leave. We're not finished.

(The actors cross to Ann.)

Don't leave me! —Okay. Go. Go. Go on. I don't need you. I was a solo performer for a long time, you know. It's a lot easier to do your own thing than dealing with a bunch of "characters" criticizing what they don't really know anything about.

B: Ann?

ANN *(Sleepy)*: Yeah?

C: Sorry to wake you. We just wanted to say good-bye.

ANN: Oh, is it over?

A: We're not really sure.

ANN: Oh. Well, it was really nice meeting all of you.

B: It was really nice meeting you, Ann.

A: Would it be okay for me to call you sometime? Or stop by? I'd love to stay in touch with you.

ANN: Well sure. I'm not too good in the mornings, but I am up all night.

(They all laugh.)

C: You are so funny!

ANN: I don't know why that's funny, but okay.

D: All right, Ann. We have to go.

ANN: All right then. You all take care.

(The actors exit, shaking their heads at Lisa as they go.)

They seemed nice.

LISA: Yeah, I guess. They were fine. You know . . . actors.

ANN: Are you okay?

LISA: Yeah. I'm fine.

ANN: Are you sure?

LISA: Yes. I'm good. I just need to take a minute to regroup. I'll be right back.

(Lisa steps into the special light. To the audience:)

I am so sorry for the confusion. We're, um, we're on track here. This whole thing is gonna come together. I just need to get past this feeling that I'm about to pass out. She and I are not going to have a confrontation here, so, please, don't worry about that. This is not about that. Don't bring your mother onstage with you. It's a very bad idea. She's not a theater person. Did I say that before? Yeah. She doesn't get how it's supposed to go. All right. I'm going to go deal with her. I'm going to calm her down, and then we'll see where we are. Wow! This avant-garde meta-theatrical thing will just bite you in your ass! Okay. Okay. I'm going to go calm her down.

(Lisa steps out of the light.)

(To Ann) Hey.

ANN: Hey.

LISA *(Looking through her note cards)*: Another . . . there's another neighborhood scene . . . I just need to figure out how to—

ANN: Do you want to just say whatever it is you're afraid to say to me?

LISA: What?

ANN: Because I'll tell you, frankly, I'd rather you just said it out loud whatever it is.

LISA: Okay. Thank you. That's good to know. I'm going to be right back.

(Ann gives a huff of frustration. Lisa steps into her special light. To the audience:)

What am I supposed to say to her!?

I went to see this guy, a few years after I moved to New York, who had been in the Allergy Unit a few years before me. This was a guy who was nearly incapacitated by his allergies. He lived in a specially outfitted RV parked in the driveway of the house where his wife and kids lived, because he was so chemically sensitive he couldn't be in his house with them for more than an hour at a time. And, as he and I talked, there came this moment where he started to register that, basically, I was telling him I wasn't sick anymore. And I'll never forget the look on his face. And he said, "How did you get better? No one gets better." It was horrible. It was horrible. And I looked down and I shrugged and I said, "I don't know." But I was thinking—it's sex. I've got this girlfriend who's cured me with sex. It's therapy. I moved to New York and got into therapy. I left Lansing and started to eat better food. I studied theater so I learned how to breathe and stretch. I learned, finally, what I never learned at home, that there is a correlation between not sleeping at night and feeling tired during the day, something I truly did not know before. I started to learn how to inhabit my body—that there is an alternative to dragging your body around like a stone and wishing it would disappear. That it is possible to integrate your physical self in with the rest of you. That the label of "allergies" doesn't work for me. That I resent that the sick people keep trying to pull me down and make me like them. That I escaped to the land of the healthy people—people who have cho-

🍂

sen strength and health and sex and attractive clothes and
organic foods and Target over Kmart even if it costs a little more—and when I come back here I want to scream:
"I AM NOT LIKE YOU!" And then I'm seized with dread
because how do I know, really, that I'm not? I think that
I've chosen to be healthy but how do I know, really, that
I won't end up in that chair like that?!

ANN: You get out of that . . . special . . . light and stay here and
deal with me.

(A stunned pause.)

LISA: Can you hear me?

ANN: Yes, of course. It's a spotlight not a sound-proof booth.

(The special light dissolves, leaving Lisa exposed in every way.)

Can you explain to me what shopping at Kmart has to do
with anything?

LISA: Kmart? . . . No, I LOVE Kmart! Oh no, did you think I was
being critical of Kmart? Oh my God. Well then you probably misinterpreted that whole thing.//Oh no. You know
what that was? . . .

ANN: I don't care about Kmart.

LISA: Okay.

ANN: I . . . I don't even know where to start. You know, I've been
sitting here and sitting here and going along with this,
even though I do not really want to be onstage, because
I like your shows—

LISA: Thank you.

ANN: —and I want you to be able to do what you need to do
but . . . Oh! Lisa, did you really bring me out here to make
people think that I'm crazy and . . . whiney . . . and a
hypochondriac?

LISA: Ummm . . .

ANN: Lisa?

LISA: I have to think about it for a minute.

ANN: Will you stop hiding behind this play and talk to me?

LISA *(To the audience)*: I don't understand what's happening. Do you? I understood this to be a very well-established theatrical device. Didn't you? I had a method. I had a plan, and if we had followed it, a pattern would have emerged. Didn't you assume a pattern was going to emerge? Yes. Because that's the way it works. Art makes sense of things, right? *(To Ann)* This is not about you and me and talking. It's about a bigger sense of making things make sense and finding a pattern that will make things make sense. Do you see what has happened because you keep interrupting?

ANN: Because you've left all sorts of important things out.

LISA: Yes! Of course I did! You can't include every single thing! *(To the audience)* It's true. I left things out. I didn't tell you, for instance, about the woman who was my roommate after Joy, who had horrible arthritis—when she came into the clinic her hands were totally knotted like this! *(Shows her fists balled-up)* And during her fast, her fingers straightened. She'd just sit there on her bed staring at her open hands. And there was an autistic girl there, about six years old. When she was cleared-out, she stopped being autistic—it happened when I was there, I saw it—and then she'd eat something she was allergic to and become autistic again. So, yes—guilty—I did. I left things out.

ANN: Why?

LISA: I don't know. Because I don't know what I'm doing! Because I should have gone to graduate school, that's why.

ANN: Lisa, I'm about ready to come over there and wring your neck//if you don't just say what you have to say to me.

LISA *(Overlapping)*: I can't. This thing has gotten//all out of proportion—

ANN *(Overlapping)*: You can—

LISA *(Overlapping)*: I can't. There's nothing—

ANN *(Overlapping)*: You're tying yourself in knots—just say what you want to say.

LISA: How can you let this happen!? WHY CAN'T YOU MAKE YOURSELF WELL?!

(*Tiny stunned pause.*)

ANN: That is a horrible question.

LISA: Well, I don't want to do this.

ANN: You have seen me struggle for years.

LISA: I know. I have.

ANN: Then what are you saying?

LISA: I was sick, too. And I got better.

ANN: And I am so grateful for that. But we are not the same person.

LISA: But, we were, Mom. We were—entwined. And that was good in a lot of ways. I mean, I understand why those actors fell in love with you—there is no place better, safer, warmer, than right up against you. That is just true. I wanted to be just like you. I imagined I would. Mom, I thought I was going to become you. I thought I was going to be a housewife and I thought I'd have kids and I'd have a house to organize and I'd have a husband, who, you know, in my case, would be away at war. I thought I was going to save a neighborhood because I couldn't imagine a life more meaningful than that. But in order to get better, I had to grow in a different direction.

ANN: Of course. You went into the Unit and you got better.

LISA: No, Mom. No.

ANN: Well then, what?

LISA: I left home and I got better.

ANN: So what you're saying is—what? You don't think you had allergies?

LISA: No, I don't think so.

ANN: Oh. Well what do you think you had?

LISA: I don't know.

ANN: Well, how do you think you got better?

LISA: I got better when I left. I got better when I went away.

ANN: What are you driving at?

LISA: I think I was sick because you were sick, Mom. I think I watched you and took for granted that it was how one lives in the world. And then I went away and learned I didn't have to be that way.

ANN: I have to process this. Lisa, I never in a million years imagined—

(A beat. Then, suddenly, the actor playing Ann—Jayne— breaks character.)

JAYNE: Wait a minute wait a minute wait a minute. *(To the audience)* I know this is jarring. I'm sorry. I need to say something.

LISA: You . . . what?

JAYNE *(To Lisa)*: I need to say something to you.

LISA: Uh—

JAYNE *(Continuing, over Lisa; to the audience, a little amazed and almost giddy at her own behavior)*: This is crazy. I'm sorry. *(To Lisa)* I have to tell you something

LISA *(Panicked that something has happened to Jayne; really asking her)*: Oh my God, Jayne, are you okay?

JAYNE: Yes, but—

LISA: What? What?

JAYNE: The ending—I can't do it. It's all wrong.

LISA: I'm sorry?

JAYNE: The ending . . . the way you wrote it . . . it's—*trite*. It's too . . . it's too—*small*.

LISA *(To the audience)*: I'm sorry. I don't . . . *(Back to Jayne)* It's fine.

JAYNE: I don't know. There's something more here. This whole thing. You're about to wrap it all up and . . . tie it together and—it's not right. I don't know what else to say. It's not right.

LISA: Jayne, I don't know what you need me to do.

JAYNE: I know. I'm sorry but— Where's that paper?

LISA: What paper?

JAYNE: I gave it to A to give to you.

LISA: This?

(Lisa hands Jayne the paper. Jayne unfolds it and looks at it.)

JAYNE: Look at this.

(Jayne hands the paper to Lisa.)

LISA *(Glancing at it, then handing it back)*: Okay.

JAYNE: Do you know what it is?

LISA: No. I don't, no.

JAYNE: Your mother wrote it. Do you know what's in those boxes? It's your mother's records from the Association.

LISA: I don't have any idea what you're trying to get at and I don't know why you're doing this, Jayne. I worked really hard on this. It took me a really long time to figure out how to make all the parts of this fit together and make it work.

JAYNE: But it doesn't work.

LISA: It does work. It was working! They were completely with us.

JAYNE: I know. But it was too easy.

LISA: No, it's not. The play is asking really hard questions.

JAYNE: I think they're the wrong questions.

LISA: They're the whole point! You don't think every person sitting there has some personal relationship to these questions? There are people out there who are sick—there are people there who are taking care of someone who's sick. We can't jerk them around. They want to know: Why are some people sick and other people get well?

JAYNE: I know they do. Questions like that are very seductive, because it would be so much easier if we could answer them. But we can't. You can't answer them.

LISA: I can.

JAYNE: You can't. Well, you *can* because you've turned this into a story that's more comfortable for you. But I think what is uncomfortable might be more . . . *(Looking for the right word)*

LISA: The purpose of this entire endeavor was to give coherence to things that are really confusing. Because otherwise it's too messy. Otherwise it's too overwhelming.

JAYNE: You mean she's too overwhelming.

LISA: Why are you pushing me like this? Jayne—yes, okay— she's overwhelming to me. That's why I wrote a play. But you're right. It doesn't work. She doesn't make any sense. She doesn't make a bit of sense as a character.

JAYNE: Oh, she does.

LISA: No, Jayne, she doesn't. She's so sick. And she's so well. I can't make her make sense.

JAYNE: That's what I'm saying. It's not about why you got better and she didn't. You keep drawing this line and putting the sick people over here and the healthy people over there. This whole play, you've been drawing a line and making sure we see that you're on one side and your mother is on the other. You're so afraid.

LISA: I'm not.

JAYNE: You're not going to become her, Lisa.

LISA: I might.

JAYNE: You won't.

LISA: How do you know?

JAYNE: Because I was the same with my mother. I loved her so much it scared me to death. I wanted to crawl right into her skin, and I couldn't push her far enough away. But, you know what? You're not going to lose yourself if you stop pushing her away. Do you know why? Because you've done it. You're separate.

Lisa, she's not the thing you've constructed in your imagination.

Be a grown-up. Take this leap. Stop fighting her. Just let her in.

LISA: I can't imagine doing that.

JAYNE: It's scary, I know. I do. But if you can do it—if you can be brave and let go of what you think you know—you'll find . . . this person. This whole other person. *(Hands her the paper)* This is a speech your mother wrote for one of the neighborhood meetings.

(Lisa reads it.)

Do you remember it?

LISA *(Nods)*: Yeah. *(Taking in the content of the speech)* Where did you find this?

JAYNE: It was right over there.

(A short beat.)

Okay. *(To the audience)* Thanks.

(Jayne exits.)

LISA *(To the audience)*: This is something my mother wrote for one of the meetings.

(She reads:)

This organization is about people. It's about busy people and lonely people. Happy people and frightened people. Young people who want a good life for their children, and old people who want to know that somebody cares. People so busy that they don't have time to wonder if anything they are doing is worthwhile, and people who face day after day of having nothing to do but wish that someone might need them. This is the purpose of integration. This is what integration means. It means weaving into the whole even the parts that are uncomfortable or don't seem to fit. Even the parts that are complicated and painful. What is more worthy of our time and our love than this?

◀ END OF PLAY

LISA KRON has been writing and performing theater in New York and around the country since coming to New York from Michigan in 1984. Her previous plays include *101 Humiliating Stories* and *2.5 Minute Ride*. Lisa is a founding member of the OBIE– and Bessie Award–winning theater company, The Five Lesbian Brothers, whose plays include *Oedipus at Palm Springs*, *Brave Smiles* and *The Secretaries*. She is the recipient of a Guggenheim Fellowship, the Cal Arts/Alpert Award, an NEA/TCG Theatre Residency Program for Playwrights fellowship and grants from Creative Capital Foundation and New York Foundation for the Arts. Her work has received OBIE, Bessie, GLAAD Media and L.A. DramaLogue awards, as well as Drama Desk and Outer Critics Circle award nominations. *2.5 Minute Ride* and *101 Humiliating Stories*, as well as the plays of The Five Lesbian Brothers, are published by TCG.